For the Scrabble
Games at the Lake!
To Carole from
Bob — Christmas 1978

POPLOLLIES AND BELLIBONES

A Celebration of Lost Words

POPLOLLIES
and
BELLIBONES
A Celebration of
Lost Words

SUSAN KELZ SPERLING

DRAWINGS BY GEORGE MORAN

Foreword by Willard R. Espy

Clarkson N. Potter, Inc., Publishers, New York
Distributed by Crown Publishers, Inc.

In memory of Boris Burac

Aimcrier

Copyright © *1977 Susan Kelz Sperling*

*All rights reserved. No part of this publication may
be reproduced, stored in a retrieval system, or trans-
mitted, in any form or by any means, electronic,
mechanical, photocopying, recording, or otherwise,
without the written permission of the publisher.
Inquiries should be addressed to Clarkson N.
Potter, Inc., One Park Avenue, New York,
N.Y. 10016*

*Published simultaneously in Canada by General
Publishing Company Limited*

First Edition

Printed in the United States of America

DESIGNED BY BETTY BINNS
ILLUSTRATIONS BY GEORGE MORAN

Library of Congress Cataloging in Publication Data

Sperling, Susan Kelz.

    Poplollies and bellibones.

    Bibliography: p.

      1. English language—Obsolete words.

2. English language—Glossaries, vocabularies, etc.

I. Title.

PE1667.S6   427   77-10547

ISBN 0-517-53079-1

Fourth Printing, March, 1978

Foreword

For several years I have kept an eye peeled for an authoritative necrology of words presumed dead. *Poplollies and Bellibones* is clearly (though in embryo, which seems odd for a necrology) the book I was waiting for. It will doubtless proceed through edition after edition, each more comprehensive than the last in vocabulary, more specific in category, more detailed in etymology. It will grow vaster—though, one hopes, less slowly—than Andrew Marvell's empires.

But let the future take care of itself. In the book as it stands, Susan Kelz Sperling has rendered a signal service. She has given us a gorgeous entertainment, redolent with smiles and chuckles for anyone who believes that words are complex beings and that sometimes it pleases them to amuse as they communicate. *Poplollies* will astonish you. It will divert you. It will instruct you. It will whet your appetite for more.

By way of starters, the author has lined up perhaps four hundred usages that were once familiar but are now forgotten. She has arranged them as if her book were a museum of natural history—in a series of dioramas, where each word is posed like a stuffed animal against a replica of its habitat, looking as if alive. A series of rounds (called garlands by the British poet Alastair Reid, originator of the form) leads the reader from one defunct word to the next, explaining each along the way until he is returned at last, exhausted but triumphant, to the place where he started. Playlets, verses, and dialogues similarly define and establish the author's poplollies in the context of their time.

There is a paradox here. Ms. Sperling reminds us that any word still in print still lives, be it available only in the most arcane lexicons and there stigmatized as obsolete, archaic, rare, dialectal, slang, or vulgar. Some of the specimens in her museum may well thrive to this day in remote hamlets of England, Scotland, Ireland, and Wales.

Even on this side of the Atlantic, a few of Ms. Sperling's choices—*widdershins* and *welkin*, for instance—remain recognizable. To be sure, they seldom appear in everyday conversation; now that witches are back in style, *widdershins* would be more likely to show up at a coven than at a cocktail party.

I spoke in my opening sentence of words presumed dead. The caveat was important. Even after being embalmed by linguists and formally laid out in their coffins for interment, words have a way of sitting up, calling for a sip of water to restore their strength, and returning as lively as ten-year-old children to their verbal rounds. *Snollygoster*, for instance, first recorded about 1865, soon went out of use again, only to be revived by President Harry S Truman, who defined it as "a man born out of wedlock." He was promptly called to account by linguistic pundits, who declared the original meaning was "shyster." However defined, *snollygoster* is back in circulation.

One cadaver memorialized in this book seems to have missed its chance at just such a triumphant return. I refer to *acersecomic*, "one whose hair is never cut." In the 1960s, when hair cascaded to the hips on male and female alike to symbolize disaffection, *acersecomic* was ripe for a second coming. Even now it must stir fretfully in its grave.

We are well rid of *floccinaucinihilipilification,* "the habit of belittling," reported here as a linkage of words from an Eton grammar of Latin. Surely this monster can never have entered the vernacular—except perhaps as a joke, like *supercalifragilisticexpialidocious,* * popularized by Walt Disney in a motion picture a few years back.

But if it would do any good, I would gladly give mouth-to-mouth resuscitation to *chantpleure,* a chiaroscuric doublet from the French meaning to sing and weep at the same time. A lovely word.

It appears that the British began very early on to transform proper names into common nouns. (They are still at it.) *Kidcote,* once generic for "prison," was named for a prison in York. A fabric from Ormuz, a city near the entrance to the Persian Gulf, was promptly termed *ormuzine.* A coarse woolen cloth called *penistone* was woven in the town of that name.

Since the author has confined herself to words that flourished hundreds of years ago in the British Isles (few in this book were born later than the seventeenth century), she has not yet had to face the dilemma of nonce terms. But if she adds to her collection, she must deal with them sooner or later. A word that was never really extant can scarcely be listed as extinct. How long must it persist before it becomes more than a passing aberration and at death is entitled to funerary rites?

---

* A correspondent reports hearing the word as early as 1926. It probably originated still earlier.

Nonce means "temporary; for the moment." The second edition of *Webster's Unabridged Dictionary* gives three examples of nonce words: *diphrelatic, decorist,* and *mammonolatry.* (Philosophers, economists, and sociologists must find themselves regularly reinventing *mammonolatry,* surely the most pervasive and enduring of America's heretic religions.)

The American Heritage Dictionary mentions but one nonce word, *mileconsuming,* used by William Faulkner in "the wagon beginning to fall into its slow and mileconsuming clatter." Dictionaries treat nonces as the work of individuals—neologisms that failed. Yet many of them spring up simultaneously and unbidden, like dandelions, through some acidifying or alkalizing of the social soil. They last until the soil changes again, and then disappear. In my childhood, *catsup,* a trade name for "ketchup," was considered, in our family, the preferred usage; yet I have not heard anyone say *catsup* for twenty years.

When Ms. Sperling shifts her sights from Britain to America, what will she do about such feisty offspring of Jacksonian democracy as *absquatulate* ("to depart stealthily"), *obflisticate* ("to obliterate"), or *ramsquaddle* ("to beat")? Each fluttered about for an hour, like a mayfly, and then perished. Should they be considered obsolete, or simply nonwords? They were born on the wrong side of the blanket, to be sure, but so were other demonic products that have survived colloquially: *bodacious, rip-roaring, rip-snorter, teetotaler, hornswoggle, shebang, shindig, skedaddle, splendiferous, spondulicks, slumgullion.*

And when did the dead words die? The vital statistics on births are mostly available, give or take a hundred years. Today we have grown comparatively precise in our dating, partly because the underground streams in which new words, especially those involving alienation, so commonly hatch; that is to say, the underworld and the counterculture are closer to the surface than they once dared be. As soon as a new locution emerges to cock a snook at society, *Time* or the *Reader's Digest* leaps on it with a glad cry and flings it into the central current of the language. But it is more difficult to be certain when a doddering word slips from public ken. It generally lingers in old reference works, sometimes with a note of the year it was first sighted:

> *Hoddypeak,* n. Simpleton,
> blockhead (1505)

How much more satisfactory if the reference encompassed the word's entire life span!

> *Hoddypeak,* n. Simpleton,
> blockhead (1505– 1733)

Perhaps Ms. Sperling will explore dates of obsoletion in her next edition.

Perhaps, too, she will uncover more of the words' life stories. The origins she does mention are as bemusing as the words themselves. To think that her titular *bellibones,* scarcely aesthetic appearing at a glance, actually means "a lovely lady, a pretty lass," and is a hobson-jobson from French *belle et bonne,* "beautiful and good"! That epiphany alone would be enough to justify this book.

Never again, alas, will we hear a crane *crunkle,* a sheep *blore,* or a donkey *winx.* Never again will we see a *shiterow* flap along a stream, though herons may abound. Nor shall I ever, however great the provocation, dare call one of my sons-in-law an *odam,* with the accent on the last syllable.

The author's device of displaying obsolete words in their original settings so intrigued me that I could not resist trying the trick myself. The result is the following *chant royal.* The theme and treatment are limited by the vocabulary at my disposal; you will find all the unfamiliar terms defined in the glossary. If you are sometimes doubtful about the pronunciation, why, so was I; simply arrange the sound of each word to fit it into the meter of the line.

CHANTPLEURE

Thought I to me, "A chant royal I'll dite—
Make much ado of words long laid away—
Wake eldnyng from bards resigned to cite
The sloomy phrases of Min Cheever's day.
I'll chantpleure, though I compass but a page;
I'll man illume, from April bud till snow,
In song all merry-go-sorry, con and pro."
I would have pulled it off, too, given time,
Had not a hidden ha-ha stubbed my toe:
Words obsolete are mighty hard to rhyme.

Ah, hadivist, in younghede, when from night
There dawned abluscent a fair morn in May
(The word for dawning, sparrow-fart, won't quite
Fit in here)—hadivist, I say,
That I'd in chair day by stoop-gallant age
Be shabbed, adushed, pitchkettled, suggilled so,
Would I have been more hoful? Yes . . . or no.
One scantling bit of outwit's all that I'm

Quite sure of, after years of catch-and-throw:
Words obsolete are mighty hard to rhyme.

In younghede, ne'er a thrip gave I for blight
Of cark or ribble—I was ycore, gay;
From hum to hum boonfellows vied, each wight
By t'others aimcried, till as one we'd sway,
Turngiddy. Blashy beer could not assuage
Such thirst, nor kill-priest, even.
                       No Lothario
Outdid my eaubruche on Poplolly Row.
The fairhead who eyebit me in my prime
Soon knew my donge. (The meaning's clear, although
Words obsolete are mighty hard to rhyme.)

Pert daggle-tails first faged my appetite;
No inwit saved me from their shittle play.
Bedswerver, likewise housebreak, was I hight—
"Poop-noddy at poop-noddy."
                      Now I pray
That other fonkins reach safe anchorage—
Find bellibone, as I did, to bestrow
The lip-clap seeds that into true-head grow;
So strewn, we fellowfeel, and scrow-ward climb.
(Frush mubblefubbles. My own climb was slow:
Words obsolete are mighty hard to rhyme.)

Now on the wong at cock-shut fails the light;
Birds' sleepy croodles cease. Not long to stay
Once nesh as open-tide, I now affright—
Am lennow, spittle-ready—samded clay,
A clutched bell-penny my remaining wage.
I wait, acclumsid. No more toward the scrow

I mount. Downsteepy is the pit below.
Ah, hadivist . . . a drumly, trantled chime.
My very outwit is malapropos:
Words obsolete are mighty hard to rhyme.

Envoy

The ghosts of blore and paggle past me blow—
The coverslut, the okselle, are *de trop*.
To lose straight-fingered phrases seems a crime.
Yet in my heart I cry, "Bravissimo!"—
Words obsolete are mighty hard to rhyme.

 My analogies in the foregoing paragraphs have generally referred to the animal kingdom. Overall, however, the comparison of obsolete words with flora may be more appropriate. Turn the page, now, and sniff the fragrance of some of the most aromatic flowers that ever faded in a British garden. This is how they were in their prime. Pluck your favorites, as I have plucked mine, and offer them as a tuzzy-muzzy to Susan Kelz Sperling.

—WILLARD R. ESPY

POPLOLLIES AND BELLIBONES

A Celebration of Lost Words

Word collecting is a chronic illness, a pleasurable malady but nonetheless impossible to cure. My first recollection of loving words for their own sake comes from the fifth grade, when the teacher subjected a friend of mine to peer ridicule for having written in a composition, "Mrs. Adams has pail blue eyes." His homophonic error made me thrill at the thought of seeing the eyes of this teacher, whom I disliked, floating helplessly in a bucket. My next symptomatic memory is of an impatient classmate, eager to break into a long line for lunch, asking me, "Where can I get ahead?"

By the eighth grade I realized that playing with words was more than a hobby. In the twelfth grade I exchanged colorful, pun-filled words with the kindred soul and teacher whose wit, whose love for language, and whose encouragement were to direct the course of my life. The writing of this book is therefore somewhat his fault; the publication of it is my eulogy to him.

Undoubtedly, my addiction/affliction is the unforeseen genetic gift of a mother and father whose native tongue was not English and who, coming from Europe, incorporated the fine and delicious subtleties of their other languages into what became their own refined patterns. Hearing other languages spoken at home by both them and my linguistically talented older sister made me aware very early of how words combine to communicate meaning. The generosity of unnamed fellow-feeling friends, professors, and former students is imprinted in these pages. The special patience and loving perseverance of a very good man and discerner of words, my husband, made this book possible. The spark of response to wordplay that my three children already exhibit is reinforcement that I had not counted on and proof that this pun-ishing chronic illness is either happily hereditary or at best contagious. You, the reader, will remain exposed to infection if you continue to ingest these pages. For the sake of the future of the English language, read on; don't quarantine yourselves. Spread the germs and let them multiply so that our disease will itself become the cure for today's sterile syntax and senseless wagging of the tongue.

Introduction

Since the dawn of language, words have been going through a process of natural selection in which only the most fit survive. Every one of us, as a reader, writer, and speaker, shapes the course of language by choosing the words we want to convey our message and rejecting those we deem inappropriate in one context or another. In short, we place value judgments on words. If this complex process of selection is multiplied by billions of people over thousands of years, it becomes apparent that language goes through an evolutionary process of its own.

All the words that are used in different ways in this book are referred to as obsolete, rare, or dialect in the various dictionaries and are seldom or never used today in writing or speech. Why, then, resurrect these words? Like an irreplaceable antique, a little-known or redis-covered word can not only be a source of pleasure in itself but may also open up fascinating insights into the past. One must not infer that because a word died, it deserved never to have lived. The sounds and meanings of these colorful dead words evoke a very alive past when these words that sound strange to us were communication tools for the people living then. Over the course of time customs changed and words associated with them fell out of use. Through this process of addition and subtraction our language evolved.

The evolution of the English language is usually divided into three major periods: Old English, from around A.D. 450 to 1150; Middle English, from around 1150 to 1500, and Modern English, from 1500 on. Invasions, wars, shifts in population, and changing lifestyles all effected changes in our language. As early as 500 B.C., Celtic invaders from the European mainland peopled the area we know now as the British Isles until more powerful Roman armies, beginning with Julius Caesar's in 55 B.C., began their conquest in search of mineral wealth and land. Over the centuries, other groups of invaders, the Irish, the Picts from Scotland, the Teutonic tribes—Saxons, Angles, Jutes, Frisians— and the Danes all left their mark on the language. In 1066, with William the Conqueror's victory over England, the heavily Germanic amalgam known as Anglo-Saxon or Old English took on French overtones and England was thrust into a new era of language consciousness.

The Renaissance of the sixteenth century, that marvelous turning point in the history of Europe, had a great impact on the English language. Travel to new lands, the rounding of the Cape of Good Hope, expeditions to the Far East, and the settling of America contributed to the exchange of ideas and a resulting influx of words into the English lexicon, as well as to the spread of English to faraway places. When the Church of England wielded its power over Catholicism during the Reformation, medieval Latin scholarship as embodied in monastic thought gave way to English. Translations of classical literature from Latin and Greek into English revived interest in words from those languages. Finally, the newly invented printing press standardized English and spread it far and wide.

The age of Elizabeth I, the true English Renaissance, epitomizes an intoxication with the arts. Word fever spread throughout the land as Elizabethan writers revived old words, coined new ones, and created the masterpieces that we moderns recognize as the body of great English literature. Shakespeare and his contemporaries played with language for the sheer pleasure of it. Their gamesmanship with words often meant using as many synonyms as one could find for one word. In the flowery 1600s a total of twenty-one words were synonyms for the "lowly" literary device we call a pun or a play on words: *bull, carriwitchet, clench, clinch, crotchet, figary, flam, jerk, liripoop, paronomasia, pundigrion, quarterquibble, quibble, quiblin, quiddity, quillet, quip, quirk, sham, whiblin,* and *whim.* A favorite pastime involved conjuring up new words by stringing together existing ones. Sometimes these inventions were exaggeratedly wind filled, as is the case with *floccinaucinihilipilification,* a word that may have been invented as a parody of its literal meaning, the habit of judging even important things as worthless.

Florid flights into verbosity went unrestrained until the eighteenth century, when academic societies during the Age of Reason met to determine taste in language. The rules of grammar and syntax were never so respected as during that time when formality, polite manners, and self-control were *de rigueur.* Purists censored words they deemed improper to use in public and others that happened to sound suspicious. Later, Romanticists rejoined with their metaphors and other figures of speech, proving that language, like other arts, mirrors the mood of the times.

We see in the twentieth century, with its fast pace and cry for incessant change, a direction toward economy in speech. Definite rules preclude casual spelling and pronunciation. Exacting people nowadays want the exact word in its exact place to get the message across with brevity and immediacy, even at the expense of grammar and originality. But word fanciers still abound.

Many of the words found herein have passed out of use because the obsolete customs, beliefs, and objects they described changed or were superseded by others. They were not universal terms, for they specifically applied only to their time.

Gone are the days of magic and health cures when a *zopissa,* a poultice of wax and pitch, would have soothed one with *agrum,* a profound swelling of the cheeks and mouth. We have come a long way from threatening naughty children with a *mumpoker* to frighten them and drive out their evil spirits. When they interrupt, we don't say, "Stop coming in with your five eggs." Fashion has forgotten the fabric *ormuzine,* once a desirable import from the Persian Gulf, and the extravagant *zendalet,* a shawl worn by Venetian women, no longer drapes over the sides of gondolas. An actor may still *blore,* bray, or bleat like an animal, and *crunkle,* cry like a crane, thereby overdoing his part, but we no longer call him a *tearcat* for his dramatic excesses.

We can rejoice that we are no longer subject to the

lovecup, a local market tax, the *swarf-penny,* money due to a castle guard when his period of service was terminated, and the *shongable,* a tax one paid for having a certain kind of shoes made. But today we could certainly benefit from the services of a *streetman,* an official appointed to oversee good government of London streets. A further loss to society is that obsolete custom of setting aside special days as *love days,* when parties were ordered by law to settle their difficulties through amicable arbitration, perhaps with the help of an *oddwoman,* the precursor of today's ombudsman.

Most by-gone punishments are best not revived, but the few to be mentioned here are too imaginative to be left in oblivion. The Old English practice called *corsned,* ordeal by exorcised bread, was the easiest of three medieval tests a prisoner underwent to determine his guilt or innocence. It called for the accused to swallow what he knew might be his last bite of food, an ounce of cheese or bread consecrated with a form of exorcism by a priest. If the morsel caused the person to become pale and go into convulsions he was deemed guilty, but if he maintained his health he was considered innocent. More horrible was the ordeal by fire, in which the prisoner was declared innocent only if a red-hot iron did not burn him. Equally severe was the ordeal by water, during which the person was bound and thrown into the water and pronounced innocent only if he sank without returning to the surface. It is hoped that the victim was retrieved in time to be exonerated.

A complement to the pillory on the village green was the *cucking-stool.* The offender, guilty of fairly harmless acts such as disorderly conduct or unfair trading practices, was fastened to a chair and jeered at by the general public or carried to a pond and dunked.

The most inventive punishment of all was the form of public derision popular through the late 1800s in parts of England, Scotland and Wales called *riding the stang*. It consisted of a procession in which an unfaithful husband was carried atop a ladder through village streets for women to censure, verbally or otherwise, at certain points along the route. A man who had beaten his wife was subjected to a slightly different mode of public ridicule. For three nights, trumpeters would rouse the villagers to join a parade, sometimes including the offender, in which the wittiest man of the town, seated in a chair strapped to poles, would be carried aloft, to the clanging of pots, pans, and horns. The mounted orator would periodically stop to proclaim a verse, such as this one recalled by William Andrews in *Old-Time Punishments:*

Here we come with a ran, dan, dang:
It's not for you, nor for me, we ride this stang;
But for——, whose wife he did bang.

Another embellishment on the practice involved burning effigies of the offenders on the village green or in front of their houses. In the ritual called *skimmington,* two performers, impersonating the husband and wife, rode through the town in a donkey cart beating each other with a ladle and skimmer, hence the name *skimmington.* They put on an especially animated performance in front of the victims' house.

Perhaps the aforementioned guilty husband had met his mistress on the havoc-filled day that people in Lancashire celebrated in the 1880s, namely *Lifting Monday.* On the Monday following Easter it was the ritual for men to lift up and kiss every woman they met. According to custom, women would reciprocate by doing likewise on Easter Tuesday, but our sources are incomplete as to whether women actually tried to lift the men. Perhaps their mutual attempt at lifting, which starts with an embrace, turned the custom into a hug. Unfortunately, these practices were short-lived because of the disturbances they caused. Some customs and the words that accompanied them are indeed better left in the dead past, but this one would be a gem to resurrect, if only for one day.

In contrast to the many obsolete words with modern synonyms, there are a number of dead words for which we have no modern equivalents, even though the obsolete words expressed timeless sentiments. What is indeed so special about these words is that they sum up in just a few syllables the eternal feelings that one often struggles at great length to find the right words for today. For example, to *chantpleure,* obviously a French contribution to our language, meant to sing and cry at the same time, perhaps at hearing a *merry-go-sorry,* a wonderful term for the kind of experience that elicits simultaneous feelings of joy and sorrow. Like the popular jokes that begin, "I have good news and bad news," a writer named Nicholas Breton wrote in 1606 in *Chance, Chance,* "Thou has told me of such a merry-go-sorry, as I have not often heard of: I am sorry for thy ill fortune, but am glad to see thee alive." Similar in spirit is the adjective *agathokakological,* a Greek term that meant possessing a combination of good and evil. Also of Greek origin are two other words lacking one-word modern equivalents, *xenodochial,* hospitable to strangers, and *philotimy,* love of honor. The singular word *storge* ("store-gee") meant the kind of love a parent would naturally feel for his children, as Thackeray used it in *Pendennis* in 1850: "I could have . . . adored in her the Divine beneficence in endowing us with the maternal storge, which . . . sanctifies the history of mankind."

Many old words describe that melancholy feeling or depression of one's spirits that one suffers for no apparent reason. One could say that he was afflicted with the *mubblefubbles* or with the *mulligrubs* or *blue devils*. If the weather remained cloudy day after day, one could complain that the sun god also was in his *mubblefubbles*. The interesting word *stoop-gallant* describes a condition that might well bring about a strong case of the *blue devils*, for it meant something that would humble a proud person. In the early sixteenth century *stoop-gallant* was the name for sweating sickness, a quick and often fatal fever that afflicted both rich and poor and therefore lowered one's pride and made him more understanding of others. A person who suffered from either the *mubblefubbles* or *stoop-gallant* sickness would have responded to the special warmth of an *aimcrier*. Derived from the role of the person who stood near the target and cried "Aim!" to direct an archer and then gave the score, *aimcrier* came to mean the kind of person who would offer approval and encouragement, bolstering another person's spirits and admiring his efforts to succeed.

A magnificent, pithy word, to *fellowfeel* meant more than to sympathize—it meant to feel in earnest how another person feels, to crawl practically under his skin to share his feelings and thereby make him feel better. *Fellowfeeling* people long ago were responsible for originating those marvelous special occasions that were respites from the busy norm, namely *Lifting Monday* and the *love days*. Such people *fellowfelt* with each other by recognizing their mutual aim of ensuring themselves a comfortable *chair day*, the evening of life when one is advanced in age and usually infirm. They thus helped prepare themselves and one another to be able to pass this time of life in peaceful ease and indulgence.

You will soon meet the old words themselves. But one word of caution before you judge their worth: be polite. These old words have waited for centuries to come up from hiding under the dust. They require patience. They look different and sound different. Speed reading would intimidate them into retreating right back under their dust jackets. They are ready for you if you treat them with respect and understanding, if you take the time to examine each on its own merits. The juxtaposition of letters in some is unusual and gives them a humorous look. The compounds are especially colorful, because the union of the two or more words into one, as with *pudding-prick, eyethurl, bellytimber, flesh-spades,* and *downsteepy,* makes us see these separate and combined words in a new light, more meaningful and fresh than before.

This is not a work in which old words are given precise definition; indeed not. Many of these words were gathered from out-of-print sources, and no further clues to corroborate their meanings could be found. Modern lexicographers can defend their interpretations of contemporary words, but since these words are dead no one can be positive about whether there is one definitive way to use them when putting them back into circulation. Many sources have varying definitions, so I have taken the liberty of choosing the ones I found most appealing. Although I use the definitions as the sources gave them, my interpretation of their original shades of meaning must be considered just that, an interpretation, and should not be taken as absolute, for there is only limited evidence to back up how to use these words today. Just as our verb *to know* can have multiple shades of meaning, such as to comprehend by means of information, to gain through inner understanding, to recognize, or to be familiar with, so can we see how difficult or misleading it is to pin down one meaning of an obsolete word as the one and only correct definition. Part of the pleasure of rediscovering these "lost beauties," as Charles Mackay referred to the words he included in his own collection one hundred years ago, comes from letting one's imagination suggest possible nuances of meaning.

I have used the words in forms that I hope will provide pleasure as well as enlightenment. What I call a round is a piece that uses up to eight words and begins and ends with the same word, a device similar to the circular canon in music. (Alastair Reid called this technique a garland in his book *Ounce, Dice, Trice.*) Stories and longer pieces include definitions of the words, some within the text, others next to it, and some elaborated more fully as footnotes. There are as well poems that may seem reminiscent of "Jabberwocky" but these obsolete words *do* have meanings, even though they may sound nonsensical at first. In the short plays, the reader is urged to consult the glossary.

Besides wishing to revive an interest in colorful words that have died, this collection hopes to make people more word conscious in general. Consider the origin of *dandelion*, a flower whose sharply indented leaves resemble *dents de lion*, lion's teeth. Take a moment to repeat simple words like *evening* and *taper*, nouns that stand for what their action verbs literally do. Evening, the time when the light of day comes together with the dark of approaching night, evens out the day with the night, and the taper, a candle, tapers off as it burns. Furthermore, anything that tapers does what a candle does: it slowly melts away. We seldom question as common a word as *breakfast,* which also is a compound word like so many of the Old English words that died. And yet it survived, perhaps because it so aptly defines the meal that breaks the period of not eating for an entire night.

Shakespeare and his contemporaries proved that inventing words can be a challenging and enjoyable pastime, especially if the new words do not merely act as fresh synonyms for existing words but truly fill gaps in our lexicon.

Since compounds like the Old English combinations that are obsolete seem particularly original and evocative upon reexamination, one might hazard a few new compound words to define ideas that lack specific terms today. Let us say that a person has exciting news that he knows it is best not to divulge right away but that he will eventually be at liberty to reveal, such as admission to a college, or pregnancy. A new compound word for the secret that one can hardly contain is *hushbuster.*

The very heart of the matter, the very core of a truth that makes a person say, "That's just what I mean!" could be termed the *pithessence.*

Someone or something that sets the all-time record for making the most money in its own category, be it a movie, an album, an entertainer, or a sports player, would be the *moneypeak* of its field.

A group of nursery school children is, of course, a *totcluster.*

It is embarrassing for a person to realize that

someone has overheard a remark he did not intend the other person to hear. The comment he wishes he could retract is a *blabblurt*.

This book is by no means complete. This very personal collection of lost words, of which there are hundreds more, is an appetizer, an invitation to sample some new words that are actually very old, savor them and, if you like, use them.

A Round of Hum

What is *hum?*
Hum is strong liquor made by combining ale or beer with spirits. Too much *hum* can make one's head *quop.*

What is *quop?*
Quop means to throb. A man's heart may *quop* with longing to hold his loved one's *feat.*

What is *feat?*
A *feat* is a dangling curl of hair. A *woup* with the *feat* of an elephant inside is considered lucky to wear.

What is a *woup?*
A *woup* is a simple metal hoop or ring not set with stones. Large *woups* to anchor one's feet could have been used at the base of a *gofe.*

What is a *gofe?*
A *gofe* is the pillory that was usually erected on the *wong,* where the greatest number of people could stroll by and see it.

What is a *wong?*
A *wong* is the meadowland that people used as
their commons, where they would meet or take
their cows to graze. Nowadays a public *wong* is
covered with *nesh* plantings and lush trees.

What is *nesh?*
Nesh means fresh, delicate, or soft, as vegetables,
foliage, or fruit should be. Braiding one's hair with
nesh flowers makes a beautiful *kell.*

What is a *kell?*
A *kell* is a woman's headdress, be it as close-set as
a net or a cap or as fancy as a wig to don for a party.
A lady's *kell* is more elaborate if she is going to a
ball where *hum* is served.

BELLYTIMBER   *Food.*

GLOP   *To swallow greedily.*

GIVEL   *To heap up.*

REELPOT   *Person who passes the drinking jug around.*

JUBBE   *Large vessel holding liquor.*

VASQUINES   *Petticoats.*

PAGGLE   *To hang loosely or bulge.*

DUMPLE   *To bend or press into a dumpy shape.*

MELPOMENISH   *Tragic, from Melpomene, the Greek muse of tragedy.*

WHOOPUBB   *Obsolete form of* hubbub, *excitement, commotion, from the Gaelic* ubub! *(an interjection of contempt) or from an ancient Irish war cry, "Abu!"*

LENNOW   *Flabby.*

PORKNELL   *Person as fat as a pig.*

EYNDILL   *Jealous.*

FAIRHEADED   *Beautiful.*

YOUNGHEDES   *Youths.*

KEAK   *To cackle, laugh at.*

FELLOWFEEL   *To share the feelings of others, sympathize with.*

NITHE   *Envy, hatred.*

TIPSYCAKES   *Cakes saturated with wine and stuck with almonds, served with custard.*

EARTHAPPLES   *Cucumbers or perhaps potatoes, which in French are* pommes de terre *("apples of the earth").*

In Praise of Bellytimber

Glop the *bellytimber, givel* the plate,
  Let the *reelpot* pass the *jubbe.*
Let *vasquines paggle* and contours *dumple,*
  'Tis not *melpomenish,* nor worth the
    whoopubb.

A *lennow porknell* might be *eyndill*
  Of *fairheaded younghedes* who *keak*
    at his paunch;
But though I *fellowfeel* with his *nithe,*
  I'd rather *tipsycakes* than *earthapples*
    for lunch.

FLAP DRAGON   *A game or sport that involved plucking raisins or other objects placed in a bowl of ignited brandy. It was not only a sign of bravado but also a point toward the lover's gallantry for him to toast the health of his lady and drain the cup without burning himself.*

FNAST   *From a noun meaning breath and related to the Greek word* pneuma *and the Old English* fnese *'snort or sneeze.'*

Tenderis the Knight:

A Medieval Misadventure

Stuff your *flatchet!*   sword
Raise your flagon!
I'm a *mildful* knight   merciful
Who'd risk *flap dragon!*   dangerous sport

sang Tenderis, the Knight, on his way to the castle of his true love, Lay Lady Lay. His horse, *Blonke, fnasted* heavily under the weight of his rider and *chamfrain.*   large horse/snorted · engraved frontlet worn by knight's horse

    "Steady on, Blonke. What a good blonke you are! Never *white-livered,* the image of *truehead,* like Rosinante. The *scrow* is getting dark now and my sight's none too keen. When we arrive at the castle I'll get you some *bellytimber* from the *acatery* while you rest in your *boose.*   cowardly · fidelity/sky · food/storeroom for provisions · cowstall

    As if in response, Blonke chomped on his

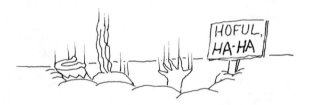

HA-HA *The kind of ditch that one could not see from a distance to avoid. Victims falling into it unaware or witnesses must have given it its fitting name.*

TO KISS THE HARE'S FOOT *An expression denoting the person who arrives so late that he misses dinner. If he comes too late to partake of the hare, his only option is* to kiss the hare's foot.

KERCHIEF-OF-PLEASANCE *The embroidered cloth presented by a lady to her knight to wear for her sake. He was bound thereby to attach it to his helmet.*

mastigadour, raised his head, lost his footing, and sank to his knees in a *ha-ha.*

    "*'Sheart!* I couldn't see that *ha-ha* in this light. Up, up with you! We must get going!" Tenderis exclaimed as he pulled on Blonke's reins. "Lay Lady Lay is waiting with her *far-net.* We daren't be late or we'll have to *kiss the hare's foot.*"

    Blonke got up slowly, trotted a few paces, and stopped, *flerking* one leg and *quetching* until Tenderis dismounted, helped Blonke to sit on his haunches, and examined the horse's leg.

    "Ah, here's the *breedbate.* A *tingle-nail* caught in your *fairney-cloots.* There! It's out. My lady's *kerchief-of-pleasance* will do for a

watering bit

ditch

An oath—"God's heart!"

company of attendants

eat scraps

jerking or twitching

uttering moans

mischief maker/tiny tack

horny substance above hoofs

embroidered cloth

ACOPON   *A soothing salve or poultice or plaster to relieve pain. In 1661 R. Lovell wrote in a medical journal that "old oil boiled to the temper and thickness of an acopon, helpeth all vices of the nerves and paines."*

WELKIN   *From the Saxon words* wealcan *'to roll' and* wolke *'a cloud'. It is also connected to the German word* wolle *'wool', used to describe the woolly quality of clouds. Shakespeare wrote in* A Midsummer Night's Dream,

> The starry *welkin* cover thee anon
> With drooping fog as black as Acheron.

bandage for now till I get an *acopon* for that
leg and some *ringo* for a treat."

poultice

sweet made from candied sea
holly root

So Tenderis helped Blonke to his feet and
walked by the horse's side in the direction of
the castle. The two made a sorry pair lumber-
ing in the dark under the weight of their garments and in their discomfort.

"Be not *swerked*, Blonke. I shall sing a
song to my lady. A lay for my Lay Lady Lay!

troubled or gloomy

> The starry *welkin* will not shine
> Till you are mine, till you are mine.
> Soon together we'll wine and dine;
> You'll drink to my love; I'll drink
>   to thine.
> A knight am I, sworn only to love,
> Never to fight, nor lay down a glove.
> We'll feather our love-nest, blessed
>   from above,
> I, Tenderis the Knight Owl, my
>   Lady, my Dove!

evening sky

Tenderis had barely spoken these words
when, neglecting to look where he was walking, he stepped right into a *drumly flosh*. Trying to regain his footing, he blindly reached
for Blonke, who lurched and unwittingly

muddy/swamp or stagnant
pool overgrown with weeds

HADIVIST!

BARLAFUMBLE *An expression a person would shout when he had fallen in wrestling or play and wanted to have a breather or time out. The word may be a corruption of the French* parlez *or the English parley.*

STOOP-GALLANT *Used here in its primary meaning, an event that would humble a vain person (make a gallant stoop). In the 1500s,* stoop-gallant *specifically referred to a fatal disease that knew no class boundaries.*

ACCLUMSID *From* clumsen, *meaning stiff or numb as though paralyzed and therefore clumsy. A Norwegian counterpart is* clumse, *meaning stiff from the cold.*

CARPET-KNIGHT *A term of contempt that applies to the knight who accomplished more on the carpet of his lady's boudoir than in battle. However, before it came to have this connotation, there was once an order called Knights of the Carpet, who were separate from those sent out to serve in the field.*

TO BREAK ONE'S STEVEN *To fail to keep an appointment. Perhaps the modern phrase "even steven" has to do with this idea of taking set turns or sharing fixed times. Steven itself also meant an outcry or the voice, especially when loud.*

adushed Tenderis's complete fall into the *sloomy* swamp.

 "*Barlafumble!* I give up! This is indeed a *stoop-gallant!* I've soaked my *purfled fewter!* Help me out, Blonke! I'll get the *gwenders* down here. What will lovely Lay Lady Lay think? Will she *snirtle* at such an *acclumsid fopdoodle?* Oh, what a knight! By now, maybe some *nott-headed carpet-knight* is lifting her *flockard* and fondling her *feat!* He

> caused
> sluggish
> call for a truce
> setback/decorated/support for lance
> tingling from cold
>
> snicker/clumsy
> fool or simpleton
> closely shorn/rake
> veil/dangling curl

could be *spuddling* about the size of his *spit-frog, shabbing* her to break her *steven* with me. I'll *suggill* him with my *snotter-clout*—

> bragging/small sword
> tricking/appointment
> beat/pocket handkerchief

NOSE OF WAX   *This term came to be used to describe an accommodating person as easily molded as wax, and was also often used to describe those who changed their faith. Roman Catholics used the term to apply to writers who interpreted the Holy Scriptures in several ways.*

MERRY-GO-SORRY   *A gem of a word that juxtaposes the two genuine emotions that one simultaneously feels when experiencing both happiness and sadness.*

PRICK-SONG   *Originally a song having all its notes (pricks) written down (pricked), not just memorized. As music became more complex and polyphonic, the term came to mean the musical line or counterpoint that accompanies the main melody.*

CHANTPLEURE   *Sing and weep at the same time.*

I'll *frush* him with my *flatchet*—for the sake   strike or crush/sword
of *philotimy!*"   honor

The woeful knight grabbed hold of
Blonke's foreleg and pulled himself out of the
water. "Ah, well, Blonke, she can't have such
a *nose of wax!* 'Tis a *merry-go-sorry* tale to   fickle personality/joyous and sad
tell. I will compose a pretty *prick-song* about   written song
the *samded* knight and his *widdershins* ad-   half-dead/unlucky
venture, one that will make her *chantpleure*   simultaneously sing and weep
and give herself to me. On we'll go, damp but
undaunted. For this knight is still young.
Pressing on, we'll lift our spirits, especially
the liquid kind, to the love of Lay Lady Lay!"

A Smellsmock's Progress

What is a *smellsmock?*
A *smellsmock* is a licentious man, perhaps a former priest, with roving eyes who often has a *paggling* stomach.

What is *paggling?*
Paggling means bulging or hanging down loosely. *Paggling* garments are worn by tired *mumpers*.

What is a *mumper?*
A *mumper* is a beggar who treks from *voil* to *voil*.

What is a *voil?*
A *voil* is a town that benefits from collecting *landcheaps*.

What is a *landcheap?*
A *landcheap* is a fine a person must pay to his lord when he leaves his land. Sometimes officials levy-

ing a *landcheap* require the services of an *oddwoman.*

What is an *oddwoman?*
An *oddwoman* is a female umpire who arbitrates heated arguments. To settle a problem, she may suggest that one party give the other an *assything.*

What is an *assything?*
An *assything* is anything one gives in compensation for an offense he has committed. Apologetic people often *faffle* when offering their assything.

What is *faffle?*
Faffle means to stammer or stumble. One might expect a woman to *faffle* in seeking to escape from a persistent *smellsmock.*

Dretching with a Fearbabe

What is a *fearbabe?*
A *fearbabe* is something a person would use intentionally to frighten a baby. One might expect a *killbuck* to make use of a fearbabe.

What is a *killbuck?*
A *killbuck* is a fierce-looking fellow who deserves a visit to a *kidcote* for his evil deeds.

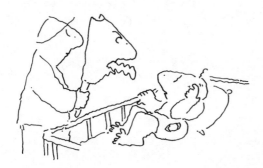

What is a *kidcote?*
A *kidcote* is a special name for a prison. Some
kidcotes don't even have an *eyethurl.*

What is an *eyethurl?*
An *eyethurl* is a window such as the one through
which the lovely Rapunzel let down her *crinets.*

What are *crinets?*
Crinets are hair. Snarled crinets can *dretch* a child
who hates to use a comb and brush.

What is *dretch?*
Dretch means to torment, as one might do with a
*fearbabe.**

* Note: For *dretching* the curly *crineted* child with a
fearbabe, the *killbuck* was sent to a *kidcote* without an
eyethurl.

SWELCHIE *A whirlpool. Also a local name for a race held in
Pentland Firth. In 1688 a J. Wallace described Orkney
Island as follows: "On the North side of the isle . . . is a
part of the Firth called the* **Swelchie** *of Stroma . . . very
dangerous."*

Young Tenderis Meets the Eerie Spirit

Before Tenderis was knighted, he endured many tests of strength and dangerous adventures. When he was six years old he had his confrontation with the much-feared Eerie Spirit, who would question him and test his courage. He had heard awful stories from *blob-tales* of how the Spirit would *agruw* boys by *yerding* them with an *elcrooked gaffle* and would then throw them into a *swelchie* if they weren't worthy of being named one of the *ycore*.

Filled with *ug*, the *younghede* Tenderis groped his way along the *downsteepy* path toward the *cosh* wherein dwelled the feared spirit-person. *Squint-a-pipes* that he was, Tenderis found negotiating his way through the *eileber* and *venenated dway-berries* very

tellers of tall tales/
horrify
beating/L-shaped
heavy metal rod
whirlpool

chosen ones

fear/youth

precipitous

hut

squinting person

plant used to cure
 liver disease
poisonous/nightshade
 berries

TEENFUL   *Causing annoyance and vexation, from the word*
teen, *meaning annoyance and irritation. In 1386 Chaucer*
wrote in his Knight's Tale,

> Never was there no word him between
> Of jealousy or any other teen.

In 1594 Shakespeare wrote in Richard III *(Act IV, Scene 1),*
"Each hour's joy wracked with a week of teen."

NABCHEAT   *From* nab *'grab, catch, pounce on' plus* cheat,
meaning an article or thing, usually stolen. Perhaps one's
hat was "the thing to grab," a "grab thing."

RECOOPER   *Getting something back, in the original sense of*
recovery. *Later,* recovery *came to mean getting back one's*
health, recuperation.

FUCUS   *A common term found in seventeenth-century*
poems. Fucus *comes from the identical word in Latin*
meaning rock lichen. Red dye was made from this lichen,
from which rouge was made. Thus "false color" or
"cosmetic paint" became the understood meaning. In 1599
Ben Jonson investigated the ingredients of fucus, *and*
Thomas Dekker suggested using fucus *to get rid of freckles.*

WANG-TOOTH   *An alternate form of* wing, *'to the side'.*
Chaucer used this word and wrote of its being situated next
to tushes *'tusks'.*

TITIVIL   *From Titivillus or Titinillus, the name that monks*
gave the devil in their mystery plays. Titivil *passed into*
popular speech undoubtedly because of its repeated use.

teenful in the *nyle.* He tripped over *zuches spiss* with *maily malshaves* that made him *quetch* at their touch. When his *nabcheat* caught on a *garfangle* hook, he did not stop to make a *redmod recooper* of it but resolved to *icchen* more *hofully* down the path.

troublesome/fog/
tree stumps/thick/
speckled/caterpillars/
shake or shiver/cap

tall plant with hooked top
hasty/recovery

move/carefully

Before he could say, "*Xiph* in a *crab-skuit,*" he found himself at the hut. What would he find inside? A *tutmouthed killbuck* with *fucus* covering his *wam,* ready to *eye-bite* him with one glance? A gigantic *verme,* a

small swordfish
open fishing boat

thick-lipped
fierce looking fellow
cosmetic paint/scar/bewitch
legendary Ganges fish
    able to destroy elephants

monstrous *rubb,* or a *trundle-tail,* with one sharp, deadly *wang-tooth?* As he slowly opened the door, Tenderis was ready to meet the devil himself. No *Adaemonist* he. This was no *fadoodle.* He expected to confront a wicked *titivil* whose *dweomercraeft* could turn him into an *irchin,* drive him to *wood-*

Greenland seal
low-bred dog
molar

nonbeliever in the
    devil
nonsense
devil who steals
    names/magic arts

hedgehog/madness

WOODNESS   *From the Old English* wud *or* wood *'out of one's mind'. In 1374 Chaucer wrote in* Troilus, *"They call love a woodness or folly."*

FIREFANGED   *An adjective applied not only to barley or cheese too hastily overheated in the oven so that it dried out but also to burning heretics at the stake.*

PUDDING-PRICK   *The thin skewer to which a bag of pudding was fastened to cook over a fire. Around 1611 it was said of one who squandered away his wealth that he "cut down a mill-post to a pudding-prick."*

FAFFLING   *Simply the echoing sound of a* faff, *a gust of wind. Therefore, to* faffle *meant to blow in sudden gusts.*

TRUCKS   *An English version of an Italian game,* trucco, *which consisted of an upright form called a king placed at one end of a table, at which the player aimed balls.*

ness, or give him the power to *rixle* like an **rule**
athel over the world. **nobleman**

But what is this? Tenderis opened the
door to find no *heanlings* huddling in **base people**
hudder-mudder, preparing to wreak havoc **secrecy**
with their *devilshine.* Instead he *istank* a **demonic powers/smelled**
firefanged smell and perceived his three older **scorched**
brothers stirring a pot, tying the *pudding-* **slender wooden skewer**
prick, and acting like *bluttering aimcriers,* **blustering/applauders**
welcoming him into the hut.

"Well done, you've done it." "You passed
the first test to knighthood!" "Stop *faffling.*" **stammering**
"Grab a *lineseat.*" "We burned the *spitch-* **stool/eel cooked**
cock and cheese, but you're no *fonkin.* Now **with bread crumbs and**
herbs/little fool
you're going to be one of us. Care for a game
of *trucks?*" **form of billiards**

Squeck, Vecke, and More

What is *squeck?*
Squeck is a disease that affects fowl. Chickens that suffer from *squeck* are miserable because they feel *yuky.*

What is *yuky?*
Yuky means itchy. A person is *yuky* if he can't get rid of *scrubbado.*

What is *scrubbado?*
Scrubbado is a term for "the itch," a long-forgotten illness cured probably by someone who, upon completing his education, was awarded his *liripoop.*

What is a *liripoop?*
A *liripoop* is the long tail that hung from a graduate's hood—the precursor of the tassel on a mortarboard. Some remarkable *veckes* nowadays return to school and earn new *liripoops.*

What is a *vecke*?
A *vecke* is an old woman. When Queen Elizabeth I became a *vecke*, she relied on *fardry* to improve her looks.

What is *fardry*?
Fardry is the act of painting one's face white. Travelling circus people practice *fardry* on each other before each performance in a *dingle*.

What is a *dingle*?
A *dingle* is a shady dell, a lowland between hills. A *dingle* would be a fine place to quarantine birds afflicted with *squeck*.

Gardyloo! Gardyloo! Thrip, Shittle, Thrip

What is *shittle?*
Shittle means unstable or inconstant. A person called a *chitty-face* may appear to be *shittle* but turn out to be really rather pleasant.

What is a *chitty-face?*
Chitty-face is a term of contempt for a person who has a thin, pinched face. Practitioners of *flerd* might look *chitty-faced* from all their sneering and selfish scheming.

What is *flerd?*
Flerd is fraud or deceit. A person would be guilty of *flerd* if he promised that using his product would get rid of *murfles.*

What are *murfles?*
Murfles are freckles. *Murfles* have caused many an attractive girl to cry on her *donge* that the fates were unkind to her.

What is a *donge*?
A *donge* is a mattress. *Farture* can make a *donge* soft or hard.

What is *farture*?
Farture is stuffing. Turkey *farture* can be made as quick as a *thrip* with modern mixes that require no baking.

What is a *thrip*?
A *thrip* is a snap of the fingers, as with the thumb and middle finger. A *thrip* hardly suffices to save a passerby if he didn't hear *"Gardyloo!"*

What is a *gardyloo*?
"Gardyloo!" is a warning cry that the people of Edinburgh in the 1770s shouted before they threw dirty water from their windows into the street. A good way to punish a *shittle* mate would be to surprise him with a *gardyloo* too late for him to escape.

ONG-TONGUE *Tattle-tale.*

BRANGLING *Noisy, wrangling.*

MUNG *A crowd of people; also chicken feed. Both definitions deal with mixing together disparate elements.*

WINXING *Braying.*

FELLY *Harshly.*

ASSYTHING *Compensation for an offense.*

Biting the Ong-tongue

If you hear, in a *brangling mung,*
You're the butt of a *winxing ong-tongue,*
   Lunge for her *felly,*
   Aim for mouth or for belly
Till you've an *assything* wrung.

What Snot Is Not

What is *snot?*
Snot is the burned part of the candle wick. *Snotty* candles would nicely illuminate supper in a *cosh.*

What is a *cosh?*
A *cosh* is a small hut or cottage to retire to after doing your daily *darg.*

What is *darg?*
Darg means a day's work. Part of a farmer's *darg* would be spent preparing *mung.*

What is *mung?*
Mung is a combination of ingredients mixed together to make chicken feed. After a fine meal of *mung* a chicken might *keak* from pleasure.

What is *keak?*
To *keak* means to cackle. Roosters who *keak* too much get *yerded* into submission.

What is *yerd?*
To *yerd* means to beat with a rod. Logs in a fireplace sometimes need a bit of *yerding* to get a fire going so that a person can *beek* in peace and quiet.

What is *beek?*
To *beek* is to bask before a fire or in the sun. *Beeking* too long in the sun can make your *pash* red and painful.

What is a *pash?*
A *pash* is a forehead. A church attendant in charge of lighting memorial candles spends a great deal of time with his *pash* over *snots.*

Roaky, Ribble, Drumly, Croodle, and Thring

Scene: *A modern office. The receptionist, Miss Fleak, is seated at desk. The telephone rings and she answers in a nasal, officious voice.*

Receptionist: Roaky, Ribble, Drumly, Croodle, and Thring.

Voice: Hello, is this the firm that deals with family law?

Recep.: Yes, sir. If you're *widdershins* in *poopnoddy,* we can *shab* you of your *mubblefubbles.* What seems to be the problem?

Voice: It's my wife. I think she's a *bedswerver.* And if this continues, it'll upset my *dillings.*

Recep.: Well, perhaps you would like to speak with Mr. Croodle. His specialty is *buck-baskets.*

Voice: I beg your pardon? I'm a bit *pitchkettled.* What did you say?

Recep.: About Mr. Croodle. He delves into the nastiest buck-baskets. That is, he'll clean your dirty linen for you, but never in public. He's a very refined man.

Voice: And how about Mr. Thring?

Recep.: Unlike Mr. Croodle, Mr. Thring loves *faries.* He and his sons—they're his favorite Thrings—love to get their *flesh-spades* into juicy *garboils.*

Voice: No, no. I just want to straighten this thing out quietly without its affecting the children.

Recep.: Well, then, perhaps Mr. Roaky could speak with you. *Storge* is his forte.

Voice: Ah, yes. I dearly love my little ones. I'm so *carked* that they'll be hurt by her *bawdreaming.* My life is completely *kew-kaw.*

Recep.: Oh, I'm so sorry. I forgot that this is *opentide,* and Mr. Roaky is away most of the day. He doesn't come in until *cockshut.*

Voice: When is Drumly in?

Recep.: Now there's a very *straight-fingered* man. Mr. Drumly puts in his *darg* from *sparrow-fart* to *dimpse*. A *kexy* fellow, but reliable and as hard-working as a *blonke*.

Voice: Fine, fine. I'll speak to him, then.

Recep.: As soon as he returns. You see, he lost his two *butter-teeth* in a fallen *scroggling* and can no longer *wheeple*. He's out getting them replaced.

Voice: So who's there for me to talk to, then?

Recep.: Well, Mr. Ribble lost his *thibble,* but if you can stay on the line he'll be back in a minute.

He's a man with a good *inwit*. He'd even give you his *assything*, his *bell-penny*, or some *chap-money* for his services.

Voice: Could you kindly go through your list of *fangers* again?

Recep.: Certainly. There's Roaky, Ribble, Drumly, Croodle, and Thring. And there's . . . *Odam.*

Voice: What?

Recep.: Not what; who. Odam is the son-in-law of Mr. Roaky. He's not as *roaky* as Mr. Ribble or as ribbled as Mr. Drumly. But then again, Mr. Drumly can be sluggish and doesn't hum along like *Croodle,* who often gets so caught up with *Thrings.* But Odam . . .

Voice: Yes, Odam! Enough of this *reak,* you *fleak!*

Thank You, Erendrake, for Your Yeresyeve

What is an *erendrake*?
An *erendrake* is a messenger whose duties might include posting *pancarts*.

What are *pancarts*?
Pancarts are public notices of the kind that announce that smoking is permitted only in the *crush-room*.

What is a *crush-room*?
A *crush-room* is the room or hall in a theatre in which the audience may gather between acts. Baroque *crush-rooms* were undoubtedly decorated with *knosps* and *ongles*.

What are *knosps* and *ongles*?
A *knosp* is an ornament in the form of a bud or a knob, whereas an *ongle* is a claw. Wood moldings of carved *knosps* and *ongles* might have surrounded a ceiling painted with a scene of Greek

gods and goddesses riding chariots across the *scrow.*

What is the *scrow?*
The *scrow* is the sky, which might inspire an artist to sketch with his *scribbet.*

What is a *scribbet?*
Scribbet is charcoal for drawing or even for dashing off a quick thank-you note for a *yeresyeve.*

What is a *yeresyeve?*
A *yeresyeve* is a gift given at the new year or upon taking office. Many a *yeresyeve* has been delivered by an *erendrake.*

52

POOP-NODDY *Fool.*

HARDHEWER *Stonemason.*

GRAFFED *Dug.*

KNOSP *Architectural ornament shaped like a bud or a knob.*

COSH *Small cottage.*

UPSY-ENGLISH *"In the manner of," "English-style."*

THEEKED *Covered a roof with protective straw.*

AIMCRY *Approve, admire.*

JUVAMENT! *"Help!"*

HADIVIST! *An expression of regret for making a mistake, a pang of remorse for having done something in ignorance, as if to say, "If I had only known!" or "I wish I had thought of it before!"*

EYETHURL *Window.*

A Poop-noddy's Mistake

The *hardhewer graffed* for stone for a *knosp*
  For the door to his *cosh, upsy-English* with burl;
He *theeked* it with thatch and stood back to
    aimcry,
    Then shrieked, *"Juvament! Hadivist!* No
eyethurl!"

Penistone Golillas

What is a *golilla?*
A *golilla* is a stiff, starched collar popular in Spain in the seventeenth century. On a Sunday outing, a Spaniard may have donned his *golilla* in search of *barilla.*

What is *barilla?*
Barilla is a water plant found in Spain and Sicily. Used in manufacturing soap, *barilla* helped to keep one's *muckender* clean.

What is a *muckender?*
A *muckender* is a bib or handkerchief easily concealed by a *coverslut.*

What is a *coverslut?*
A *coverslut* is an apron or any garment intended to conceal slovenliness. Yorkshiremen wore *penistone coversluts.*

What is *penistone?*
Penistone is a coarse cloth named after the York-shire town of Penistone (pronounced "Pennystun") where it was made. Hand-woven goods made of *penistone* cloth may have won prizes at the fair where *bartholomew-pig* was one of the main attractions.

What is *bartholomew-pig?*
Bartholomew-pig is the roasted pig displayed and eaten each year at the Bartholomew Fair in London. A person who ate too much *bartholomew-pig* paid for his excesses at a local *spittle.*

What is a *spittle?*
A *spittle* is an almshouse or hospital where the all-purpose panacea was a dose of *slibber-sauce.*

What is *slibber-sauce?*
Slibber-sauce is the slang term for a nauseating concoction usually given for medicinal purposes. If *slibber-sauce* was particularly distasteful, a re-calcitrant patient might spit it out and stain his *golilla.*

BELLIBONE *A whimsically anatomical word, an anglicized version of the French expression* belle et bonne *'a fair lass'.*

SANAP *From the Old French* sauvenape *'save the nape' (tablecloth). This particular strip of cloth was placed over the outer edges of the tablecloth to keep it from being soiled.*

TENTERBELLIES *Fat persons. We no longer refer to a* tenter, *a wooden framework on which to stretch cloth so it will not shrink, but do speak of being on tenterhooks, tensely hanging there at the edge of knowing something.* Tenterbellies *therefore means "stretchbellies," people with bellies distended as cloth attached to hooks would be.*

Tenderis's Quest for Romance

Having proved himself on the battlefield, Tenderis's heart *quopped* with the thrill of meeting a different sort of challenge. He vowed to *rixle* over the affections of the latest *bellibone* to catch his fancy, *fairheaded* Pretty Pure Polly Esther. He had *yarkened* a picnic for them to share in a picturesque spot just a *wurp* away from a *brooling* brook, where Tenderis grandly unfolded the *sanap* for their lunch.

"There's so much to eat!" exclaimed Polly Esther. "We'll gorge ourselves like *tenterbellies*! *Nesh earthapples* and *fasels* too! Tenderis, help me with this heavy *jubbe* and *zegedines*."

"Of course, my lovely Polly. You could *fage* the stars to shine all day. How *mally* I

throbbed or palpitated

rule or have dominion

pretty girl/beautiful

prepared

stone's throw/murmuring

protective cloth

gluttons

fresh/cucumbers
chick-peas and kidney beans
large pitcher

drinking cups

coax/foolishly fond

BACKSTRESS *The female counterpart to* backster, *the forerunner of* baker *and the old spelling of* Baxter, *one of many proper names derived from occupations, such as Cooper and Warden.*

ROBERDAVY *A specific kind of wine consumed in the sixteenth and seventeenth centuries. Since we do not know how it got its name, one can only conjecture that a Robert and a Davy or a Robert Davy thereby achieved immortality.*

ZARF *From the Arabic word for vessel. A* zarf *is a cup made of ornamented metal, as well as a cup-shaped holder for hot coffee.*

BUMBO *A delicious punch made by combining rum, sugar, nutmeg, and water. Its name is borrowed from the word that Italian children use for* drink.

am of you! Taste some of this *bellytimber* I brought. There's no *maw-wallop* here. But," said Tenderis, "I'll just have a bite of the bread I've bought from the *backstress* and wash it down with some *roberdavy*. Fill my *zarf* to the brim and I'll drink in your captivating *wink-a-peeps*."

    "Be *hoful*, Tenderis. That wine might be as strong as *hum* from being out in the warm sun."

    "Don't you worry, my Pretty Polly. The *reelpot* at the *kidliwink* promised me this wine is light as *aleberry*. Come on. Have some. It's mild, not even as sweet as your *bumbo*. It's so *blashy* it's almost like *Adam's*

food

badly cooked mess of food

female baker

wine

cup

eyes

careful

strong mixture of ale or beer and spirits

tavern keeper or bartender
beer shop or *tidliwink*
ale with sugar, spices and bread sops

rum punch/thin and weak

ADAM'S ALE *A humorous reference to the fact that the only drink that Adam and Eve had available to them was water.*

CONDOG *To concur. An inventive punster must have enjoyed playing with the second syllable by substituting the synonym* dog *for* cur.

POPLOLLY *An affectionate term that comes from the French* poupelet *'little darling' and that came to be applied to a mistress.*

ale. I could drink ten glasses and never feel a   water
thing."

He proffered his cup to Polly Esther.
"Why, I don't *condog* with you at all, Ten-   agree
deris. This tastes as strong as *kill-priest* to   port wine
me. Maybe that *reelpot* is really a *nickpot*   bartender
who gave you *merry-go-down* instead."   fraudulent innkeeper
strong ale

"Now, don't be *carked,* Polly. Just let   fretfully anxious
your mind *dringle* while I drain this one cup   idle lazily
more, and I'll sing you a song." Tenderis,
holding his cup as if in a toast, sang:

Please, please, Pretty Pure Polly,
Please me. Prithee, be my *poplolly;*   little darling or
Pretty please, O Pretty Polly,   a mistress
'Twould be forever, not for folly.

Wouldst I had this Polly Esther,
My love pain, it would not fester;
I'd adore her, never test her,
Be her knight, and not a jester.

No misfortune grand or slight
Can obscure the future bright
For sweet Polly and her knight,
Valiant by day and tender by night.

PISSABED   *The term given to the dandelion because of its effect on urine or urination; sources are unclear as to which. A gentleman named T. Lewis Davies wrote, "Wolcot in a note says that the second Lord Chatham was named F.R.S. for presenting some such plant to the Royal Society." Not everyone was in agreement with bestowing membership in the Select Society to Chatham, for a P. Pindar wrote:*

> Through him each trifle-hunter that can bring
> A grub, a weed, a moth, a beetle's wing,
> Shall, to a Fellow's dignity succeed;
> Witness L.C. and his piss-a-bed.

LIRIPOOP   *A word with many meanings, its oldest being the long tail that was once part of clerical dress. Later it became part of a graduate's hood and the forerunner of the tassel on a mortarboard. Both meanings could have come from the Latin* cleropeplus *'livery hood'. By the time of Edward III, a* liripoop *came to be a scarf that men donned when dressing extravagantly. As a result of its connection with a graduate, a* liripoop *also came to mean something that had to be learned, like a role or part, as the word is used in this story. A person referred to as one who knows his* liripoop *was considered knowledgeable enough to be entitled to wear the scarf or doctoral hood of the Sorbonne, for example. Still further, Beaumont and Fletcher used the word in* Wit at Several Weapons *to mean a verbal trick, from another term,* lerry-word. *And it has been said that in Devon people use the word to denote a silly person.*

Tenderis reached into the bottom of the picnic basket and began *sparpling* a few *lulibibs* and *kissing-comfits*. "Sweets for the sweet, Polly Esther."

scattering

lollipops/sugar candy or breath sweeteners

He leaned toward Polly for a *lip-clap* but, slightly *turngiddy*, he toppled forward, sprawled on his love, and ended up eye to eye with a *pissabed*.

kiss

dizzy

dandelion

"Tenderis! You *breedbate!* You've knocked me over!" cried Polly Esther, struggling to raise herself up and rearrange her clothing. "You sang such a sweet *liripoop*. Why did you have to spoil it with a *mulwine?*"

mischief-maker

recitation or part

drinking bout

VECKE   *Possibly from the Italian* vecchia, *the feminine form of* vecchio *'old'. The* Oxford English Dictionary *qualifies its granting this derivation by explaining, "As direct adoption from Italian would be remarkable in the fourteenth century, it is possible that the word existed in Old French colloquial use."*

"Oh, don't be a silly *vecke!*" replied Tenderis. "Do you really think I'm so *feather-headed* that I can't hold my cups?" He quickly stood up. "I'm not *turngiddy*. Come, let's make a *hand-band*."

old woman

scatterbrained

dizzy

covenant made by joining hands

She let Tenderis take her hand, into which he thrust a *tisty-tosty* of *bunnikins*. "Will this *lovedrury* of mine convince you to have a *mentimutation?*" he asked.

nosegay
early spring flowers
love token, keepsake

change of mind

Polly laughed. "You are filled with surprises, Tenderis. Whenever I'm with you, I never know what'll *ilimp* next. How can I be *thrunch* at someone as *iqueme* as you?"

happen

angry/pleasing, agreeable

Tenderis plucked one *bunnikin* from her *tuzzy-muzzy* and, picking the petals from the flower, sang, "She loves me. She loves me not. She loves me . . . ."

flower

nosegay

SNAWKY   *Nauseating.*

LUBBER-WORT   *Food of no nutritive value, "junk food."*

RUTTERKIN   *Swaggering boor.*

DINGLE   *Shady dell between hills.*

DRETCHING   *Tormenting.*

THEOW   *Servant.*

DRINGLE   *To waste time lazily.*

CRUG   *Food. In its original use in the early 1800s at Christ's Hospital School in Hertford, England, it referred to the measly crusts of bread that poor victims there dipped into beer to get some nourishment and taste.*

SLIBBER-SAUCE   *Concoctions, especially those used as medicine.*

PINGLE   *To eat with little or no appetite.*

Snawky Lubber-wort

A *rutterkin* lived in a *dingle*,
Dretching his *theow*, who would *dringle*,
  "Your *crug*'s no great loss,
  Nor your *snawky slibber-sauce*.
Such *lubber-wort* just makes me *pingle!*"

Theeking Shiterows

What is a *shiterow*?
A *shiterow* is a heron who might choose to *theek* her nesting place so no one could steal her eggs.

What is *theek*?
To *theek* means to cover and, in general, protect something. Specifically, it means to cover a roof with straw thatch. In any given *begler-beglic*, people *theeked* their homes in many different styles and patterns.

What is a *begler-beglic*?
A *begler-beglic* is the district over which ruled a *begler-beg*, the governor of a province within the Ottoman Empire. Ranked next to the grand vizier, the *begler-beg* probably had a personal servant to trim his *bugle-beard*.

What is a *bugle-beard*?
A *bugle-beard* is a shaggy beard resembling buffalo hair. A *yetter* should avoid growing a *bugle-beard* or it could get in the way of his work.

What is a *yetter?*
A *yetter* is a metal-caster whose specialized job might be casting the cylindrical molds for *ataballes.*

What are *ataballes?*
Ataballes are kettle-drums, otherwise known as "smurd" in *back-slang.*

What is *back-slang?*
Back-slang is the technique of saying words backwards. One can be showy and toss off a polysyllabic word like "noitacirbulibom" or be modest and settle for two syllables with "gnil-reps" which is *back-slang* for *sperling.*

What is a *sperling?*
A *sperling* is a small, common European smelt as well as a young American herring. While hoping to catch a *sperling*, a quiet fisherman may be lucky enough to spot a *shiterow.*

A Walk through the *Wong*

Miss Fleak, formerly the receptionist of Roaky, Ribble, Drumly, Croodle and Thring, has a new position as one of the operators on the answering service for the police headquarters.

Caller: Hello! Police? My *trantles* have been stolen!

Fleak: I am sorry, sir, but all the officers are out celebrating at their *bean-feast.* This is the answering service. May I help you?

Caller: No! I don't want to talk to some *afterling!* I want the chief of police!

Fleak: I told you, sir, he's out *glopping* his *bellytimber.* When he returns, I'll give him your message.

Caller: Yes, yes, all right. Please write everything down. I don't want anyone to *misgloze* what happened to me.

Fleak: Certainly. I'll take down every word.

Caller: You see, I was on my way out of town, carrying my suitcase filled with all of my most valuable possessions. Some people might call them *trantles,* but to me they mean a lot.

Fleak: Oh, I know what you mean, sir. My handbag is like a *bulse* to me.

Caller: Well, I took a short-cut through the Boston *Wong.*

Fleak: Through Boston Wong? Oh, it's so lovely there! The *nesh* flowers in spring, the *shiterows* in the river . . .

Caller: Miss! Are you listening? I'm telling you a *melpomenish* story and you're talking *fadoodle!*

Fleak: Sorry, sir. You were saying about the Wong?"

Caller: The trees were *purfled* with snow and I stopped for a minute and put down my suitcase, mind you, for just one instant, to watch a few children *hurley-hacket* before *cockshut.*

Fleak: Sorry to interrupt, sir, but I seem to have dropped my *dentiscalp* and I'm . . . looking . . . around . . . Ah! Here it is. Go on, sir.

Caller: My suitcase! It was suddenly gone!

Fleak: Gone? Where did you lose it?

Caller: How can you ask me that? I didn't lose it—someone stole it! I just hope you're *pricking* this down! You don't seem to understand! Someone sneaked up on me and . . .

Fleak: Are you sure? You know, you can't just call everyone you meet a *wind-sucker.*

Caller: Some *yisser* made off with my luggage. That's why I'm calling the police! If there were more *streetmen* around, this never would have happened!

Fleak: Quite right, sir, right you are. Why, one day I opened my *bubble-bow* to give a *mumper* some *chinkers* just to get him to stop *thigging,* and he upped and grabbed the whole bubble-bow, and ran off!

Caller: And those cops right now are out at their bean-feast while *magsmen* are practicing *figging-law* all over town!

Fleak: Now really, sir, some charity, if you please! All of our officers are decent men, no *gattoothed rutterkins,* and the chief won't allow any *acerse-*

comics on his force, no sir! And none of them has ever been caught collecting *dead pay,* either.

Caller: Okay, okay. I looked around me for the culprit. And sure enough, in the distance I saw the thief or his *cloyer tittuping* through the snow with my suitcase tucked under his *okselle.*

Fleak: Right or left?

Caller: Right or left what?

Fleak: Okselle, sir.

Caller: What difference does that make?

Fleak: I just want to get down all the facts, sir. Did you run after him?

Caller: Of course! But he ducked into an alley. It was already *dimpse* and the sun had gone down.

And I lost sight of him. I found only a small *yep-sen* of change in my pocket, so I called you.

Fleak: Good thinking. Can you give me a description of the thief?

Caller: I never saw him close enough. He was fast. He must have done quite a bit of *snapsauce* when he was very young and gone on from there. I hope for his sake he's *flag-fallen* and maybe getting some things he needs from my loss and isn't just a prankster who plays *bubble-the-justice* for a lark.

Fleak: Now what was inside your suitcase?

Caller: Everything I've ever *iswonken* for! All my clothes. But that's nothing compared to having lost my little treasures, my one-and-only *liripoop!*

Fleak: Your liripoop! That is a great loss.

Caller: And my silver *orlings!* Irreplaceable! I hope my *golilla* gives him *merry-galls!*

Fleak: Silver orlings . . . did you say *golilla?*

Caller: Yes, handmade from only the finest cloth. Fie on his needs! *Whisterpoops* are too good for the scoundrel!

Fleak: Whisterpoops . . .

Caller: No, no! That doesn't go on the list! Am I *umbecast* by incompetents? Why are there no magistrates when you need them? Why must I get an operator who's a *fleak?*

Fleak: Why, yes! I'm Miss Fleak. How clever of you to know my name!

Caller: Oh! It's my luck to be plugged in to you!

Fleak: Why, thank you! And please go on with your story. It's so exciting! Can you hear me? Is there something wrong with our connection? Hello . . . Hello! . . . Oh, I seem to have lost him . . . such a nice man. He remembered me and I never even got his name or number!

Presenting the Prickmedainty

What is a *prickmedainty*?

A *prickmedainty* is a dandy, a person who is very finicky about his or her style of dress. Female *prickmedainties* apply *calliblephary* as the final pièce de résistance.

What is *calliblephary?*
Calliblephary is coloring for the eyelids. Only *dweomercraeft* can transform an ugly hag, who can't expect *calliblephary* to make her irresistible.

What is *dweomercraeft?*
Dweomercraeft is the art of magic or juggling. A star performer of *dweomercraeft* whose fame has gone to his head may lose all his appeal by exhibiting and expecting gross *pumpkinification* in public.

What is *pumpkinification?*
Pumpkinification is exaggerated praise or pompous behavior. Like any other human quality, *pumpkinification* can be *agathokakological* to one's self-image.

What is *agathokakological?*
Agathokakological means comprised of good and evil. If one's *agathokakological* balance is weighted to one side, one might resort to leveling *whistersnefets* at an adversary during an argument.

What are *whistersnefets?*
A *whistersnefet* is a blow or buffet, like a slap on the ear. Whistersnefets are a source of *adlubescence* for masochists.

What is *adlubescence?*
Adlubescence means pleasure or delight. If consummate *adlubescence* is your only quest you

might spurn the little pleasures of life and fall victim to *floccinaucinihilipilification.*

What is *floccinaucinihilipilification?* *Floccinaucinihilipilification* is the habit of belittling achievements of others. A jealous cynic may indulge in *floccinaucinihilipilification,* belittling the painstaking efforts another has made in maintaining his reputation as a *prickmedainty.*

Name Calling

The popular sport of name calling has probably existed since the beginning of time. When one looks over the wealth of choice derogatory terms that are now defunct, one decries this loss. The obsolete words seem to be aimed at people in four categories: base, contemptible persons and bullying braggarts; fat, greedy people; fools; women.

Base, contemptible persons and bullying braggarts

Consider the mileage to be gained from calling an adversary not just contemptible but a *mumper, lickspittle,* or *lickspigot.* These names are akin in that the *mumper* begged and sponged off others, whereas the *lickspittle* or *lickspigot* was an even more revolting parasite who hung on, even to lick the last drop from a spigot.

Hoodpick and *giveler* are related in that the *hoodpick,* a miser or skinflint, was one degree above the *giveler,* who probably deserved this term of contempt for his avaricious habit of hoarding things for himself.

A *heanling* was a low, base person, the kind you wouldn't give a second thought to kicking aside, whereas a *whifling* was so onomatopoetically insignificant as to be worthy of being called practically nothing at all.

A *killbuck* resembled a *killcow* in one respect only: both looked fierce enough to terrorize—to cow—another person. But the term *killcow* went further. It applied also to a murder-

ous type of fellow, a real butcher, of the notorious kind that inspired this ballad from the 1600s advising against becoming a meat dealer:

Of all occupations that nowadays are used
I would not be a butcher, for that's to be
    refused;
For whatever is gotten, or whatever is gained,
He shall be called killcow, and so shall be
    named.

Killcow was also the term for a person who thought he was a somebody, a braggart who earned his sobriquet by intimidating helpless women who, like cows, were unwarlike, placid creatures and therefore easy to bully. This type of killcow was comparable to the swaggering swashbuckler known as a *rutterkin,* for both were full of their own inflated self-images and were worthy of such windy-sounding nicknames as *huff-muff, huff-snuff, huff-nose,* and *hufty-tufty.*

Be he *killcow, killbuck,* or *rutterkin,* the *waghalter* went beyond swashbuckling, threatening, and terrorizing; he deserved to *wag* 'swing' on the *halter* 'gallows', for having committed an evil offense.

Not merely a licentious man, the term smellsmock referred as early as 1550 to an errant clergyman. In 1634 a gentleman named Thomas Heywood wrote in his book *Maidenhead, Well Lost,* "I think you'll prove little better than a *smellsmock,* that can find out a pretty wench in such a corner." One can therefore deduce a double interpretation of the word. The term *smellsmock* would apply not only to a man of God whose extra-curricular activities gave him a smelly smock but also to a lecherous womanizer who knew how to "smell a smock," that is, to recognize an easy conquest.

Fat, greedy people

Gluttons were guilty of *aletude,* fatness of the body. A person we might call gross today used to be called such terms as *porknell, gundygut, greedigut,* or *tenterbelly.*

The *porknell* was, as the term implies, as fat as a pig. *Gundygut* and *greedigut* carried more derogatory overtones and characterized the person who ate voraciously, offensively, and with no manners at all. The *tenterbelly* was one who had his stomach literally stretched to its farthest capacity, as cloth was formerly stretched on hooks.

Fools

Fools have always been around for others' pleasure, but they are no longer designated by such lively names as *fopdoodle,* a word for an ordinary simpleton or fool. *Fonkin* was a diminutive, almost affectionate-sounding word for a little fool who possessed more charm perhaps than the silly *fopdoodle.*

A *hoddypeak* was a stupid blockhead, as were the *hoddy-noddy* and the *hoddypoll.*

Interestingly enough, the term *poop-noddy* meant not only a fool but also the game of love, in which most people might become giddy or silly.

The simple fool who proved himself to be "soft in the head" was nicknamed *velvet head* and was thereby compared to a young deer whose horns were still covered with soft velvet.

And, finally, the fool who was called a *mobard* was the kind of clown who was more boorish than amusing.

Women

Women seemed especially vulnerable as targets and were most definitely not exempt from insult. Probably some early terms for certain kinds of women are extinct because standards of taste deemed them unprintable. A few that remain are *fleak, tirliry-puffkin,* and *fizgig.*

The two dialogues in this book feature Miss Fleak, a not-too-bright insignificant creature who exemplifies her name. She might also have been called a *tirliry-puffkin,* the term for a lightheaded, flighty woman. More dizzy and frivolous was the *fizgig,* a woman who, without her *gig,* or senses about her, flew off in different directions, like the fizzing paper firework of the same name.

A woman was termed *fliperous* if she was both a minx and a proud gossip. Proud in demeanor also, the *tittup* paraded about by walking with an up-and-down movement like the prancing of a horse, the sound of whose feet while cantering was "tittup, tittup." But who is to say whether or not the pun implicit in this onomatopoetic term for a forward hussy is truly unintentional?

Wallydraigle, drassock, and daggle-tail or draggle-tail are three names that apply to a slovenly woman. Both the wallydraigle and the drassock were drab, unkempt, untidy, and worthless women, whereas the daggle-tail or draggle-tail wore garments that became sloppy and dirty by their being trailed over wet ground.

It is only a short step from a woman's wearing filthy skirts to her being called a slut, as the daggle-tail and others came to be called. The slovenly drossell, whose epithet had as many variations (drotchell, dratchell, drazell) as a musical piece, was exploited as crassly as the taw-bess, another name for a slattern. The male who called a woman the abusive term whipperginnie revealed himself to be an outright user of women, for this term, like whip-her-jenny, conveyed his disrespect for her and his disregard for her right to retain her virginity. Curiously, the word eventually became the name of a card game and the phrase "land of whipperginnie" a nickname for purgatory.

Older women as well were accorded special words showing contempt. The *bronstrops* or *bawdstrot* was not only a prostitute but also a procuress. To call a woman a *walking mort* was the ultimate insult. Like "moving death," she was a despicable sight—a grown-up, unmarried whore who often pretended to be a widow, acting out a transparent charade.

Not all names were derogatory of course. A man who had a favorite mistress might have playfully referred to her as his *poplolly,* from the French *poupelet* 'darling' and have paid her a compliment by calling her a *bellibone.* A corruption of the French adjectival phrase *belle et bonne* 'fair and good', the term meant a fair maid or a bonny (perhaps from *bonne* again) lass. Let's not forget the *boonfellow,* a warm companion, or those people who expressed their *merry-go-sorry* feelings, mixed feelings of joy and sorrow. *Fellow-feelers* did exist. But the derisive terms seem somehow more prevalent—and a lot more fun.

Glossary

Aids to pronunciation are given where necessary and when available.

ACATERY   Around the year 1400, provisions purchased for a king as well as the name of the room in which they are stored. *Acatery* derived from French *acheter* 'to buy'. The officers in charge of an *acatery* were a sergeant, two joint clerks, and yeomen who supervised meat, grain, delicacies, and salt.

ACCLUMSID   Numbed, paralyzed, clumsy. From the Old English *clumsen* 'to be stiff, numb'.

ACERSECOMIC   One whose hair was never cut. From the Greek.

ACOPON   A soothing salve, poultice, or plaster to relieve pain.

ADAEMONIST   A person who denies belief in the devil.

ADAM'S ALE   A humorous term for water, the only drink for Adam and Eve.

ADLUBESCENCE (accent on *bes*)   Pleasure, delight.

ADUSH (accent on *ush*)   To cause to fall heavily, to precipitate.

AFTERLING   An inferior.

AGATHOKAKOLOGICAL (accent on *log*)   With a mingling of good and evil.

AGRUM   A swelling of the cheeks or mouth.

AGRUW (accent on *gruw*)   To horrify, to cause shuddering.

AIMCRIER   An applauder, encourager, the person who cried "Aim!" to encourage an archer; the one who stood near the target to report the results of each round.

ALEBERRY   Ale boiled with spices, sugar, and sops of bread.

ALETUDE   Obesity, bodily fatness.

ASSYTHING   (accent on *syth*, pronounced *sithe*)   Something given as compensation for an offense; reparations.

ATABALLES   Kettle-drums.

ATHEL (accent on *a*)   A nobleman.

BACK-SLANG   The technique of pronouncing words backwards.

BACKSTRESS   A female baker.

BARILLA (accent on *rill*)   A marine plant from Spain and Sicily used in manufacturing soap.

BARLAFUMBLE   A call for a truce by a person who has fallen in play or wrestling; a request for time out.

BARTHOLOMEW-PIG   Roasted pig displayed and eaten at

the annual Bartholomew Fair on Saint Bartholomew's Day, August 24, from 1133 to 1855, in London. Shakespeare used it as a derisive term for Falstaff.

BAWDREAMING   Bawdy misbehavior.

BAWDSTROT.   See *bronstrops.*

BEAN-FEAST   An annual dinner given by employers for their workers in the late 1800s in England. Its name comes from the appearance of beans at the table or the serving of a bean goose whose bill resembled a horse-bean. It is possible also that the name comes from the Middle English word *bene* 'prayer, solicitation', since it was the custom to solicit or take up collections for the common good at that occasion.

BEDSWERVER   A person unfaithful to the marriage bed. Synonym: *spousebreak.*

BEEK   To bask in the sun or before a fire.

BEGLER-BEGLIC   A district over which ruled a *begler-beg,* the governor of a province in the Ottoman Empire, who ranked next to the grand vizier.

BELLIBONE   A lovely maiden, a pretty lass. An anglicization of the French *belle et bonne* 'fair and good'.

BELL-PENNY   Money one saves for his own funeral.

BELLYTIMBER   Food, provisions.

BLASHY   Thin or weak, as applied to tea or beer.

BLOB-TALE   A tattle-tale or gossip. Synonym: *ong-tongue.*

BLONKE   A large, powerful horse.

BLORE   To cry out or bleat and bray like an animal.

BLUTTER   To blurt out.

BOONFELLOW   A warm companion.

BOOSE   A cow stall.

BRANGLE   Verb: to squabble or brawl; noun: a muddle or state of confusion.

BREEDBATE   A person or something that creates strife; a mischief maker.

BRONSTROPS   A prostitute.

BROOL   A low, deep humming, a murmur.

BUBBLE-BOW   A lady's tweezer box or pocketbook. Perhaps originally a misspelling of *bauble-buoy,* a container for baubles.

BUBBLE-THE-JUSTICE   "Cheat the magistrate"—a nineteenth-century game of nine holes. From *bubble* 'dupe'.

BUCK-BASKET   A large basket to carry dirty linen. From *buck* 'bleach' and Celtic *buac,* cow dung mixed with other materials to make lye for bleaching linen.

BUGLE-BEARD   A shaggy beard like buffalo hair.

BULSE   A package of diamonds or gold dust. The word comes from the medieval Latin *bursa* 'purse'.

BUMBO   Italian, a child's word for *drink;* a punch made of rum, sugar, water, and nutmeg.

BUTTER-TEETH   The two upper middle incisors.

CALLIBLEPHARY (accent on *bleph*)   A coloring for eyelids. From the Greek words *kallos* 'beauty' and *belepharon* 'eyelid'.

CARKED   Fretfully anxious.

CARPET-KNIGHT   A derogatory term for a knight who achieved more on the carpet of a lady's boudoir than in battle; the Knights of the Carpet, an order of knights so called to distinguish them from those who served in the field.

CHAIR DAY   The evening of life, that time when a person is old and usually infirm but passes his time in ease and comfort.

CHAMFRAIN   The frontlet of an armed horse for a feudal knight, often engraved with designs.

CHANTPLEURE   To sing and weep at the same time.

CHAP-MONEY   Small sums returned to the buyer when he pays for a purchase—a discount. From Old English *ceap* 'barter, deal'. A *chapman* was one who made deals.

CHINKERS   Money, coins.

CHITTY-FACE   A person with a thin, pinched face; a term of contempt.

CLOYER   A pickpocket's accomplice or the one who intrudes into a bunch of thieves to claim a share.

COCKSHUT   Twilight; the time poultry are shut up for the night.

CONDOG   To agree; a pun on *concur.*

CORSNED   The ordeal by bread, a medieval test to determine guilt. The accused was ordered to swallow an ounce of bread consecrated by a priest with an exorcism. If he went into convulsions he was pronounced guilty, but if he had no reaction he was proclaimed innocent. From the Old English *cor* 'trial' and *snaed* 'piece'.

COSH   A small cottage, hut.

COVERSLUT   An apron; an architectural decoration to cover ugliness or deformity.

CRAB-SKUIT   A small, open fishing boat with sails.

CRINET   A hair.

CROODLE   To creep close; a faint humming, the low music of birds.

CRUG   Food (slang), from crusts of bread at Christ's Hospital School in Hertford, England, dipped in beer to add taste.

CRUNKLE   To cry like a crane.

CRUSH-ROOM   A room or hall in a theatre in which the audience could stroll between acts.

CUCKING-STOOL   A chair for punishment in which the offender was fastened, to be jeered at publicly or dunked in a lake or river.

DAGGLE-TAIL   A woman whose garments are dirtied by being trailed over wet ground, so by extension an untidy woman, a slut or slattern.

DARG   A day's work.

DEAD PAY   Pay continued to a dead soldier that is taken by dishonest officers for themselves.

DENTISCALP   A toothpick. From the Latin *dens* 'tooth' and *scalpere* 'to scratch'.

DEVILSHINE   Demonic power or skill.

DILLING   A child born when the parents are old; possibly a corruption of *darling; dilling-pig,* the weakling in a litter.

DIMPSE   The dimming of daylight, twilight. See also *cockshut.*

DINGLE   A shaded dell, a hollow between hills. Also *dimble, dumble.*

DONGE   A mattress.

DOWNSTEEPY   Steeply descending, precipitous.

DRAGGLE-TAIL   See *daggle-tail.*

DRASSOCK   A drab, untidy woman.

DRETCH   To torment.

DRINGLE   To waste time in a lazy manner. Also *drubble, drumble.*

DROSSELL   A slut, hussy. Also *drazell.*

DRUMLY   Cloudy, sluggish. From Old English *droum* 'mud'.

DUMPLE   To bend or compress into a dumpy shape.

DWAY-BERRY   The berry of the deadly nightshade, resembling black cherries.

DWEOMERCRAEFT (accent on *o*)   Juggling, the magic arts.

EARTHAPPLE   A cucumber or potato. Perhaps from the French *pomme de terre* 'potato', literally "apple of the earth."

EAUBRUCHE   Adultery.

EILEBER   A plant used as a remedy for liver disease and lumbago.

ELCROOKED   L-shaped.

ELDNYNG   Jealousy, suspicion.

ERENDRAKE   A messenger.

EYEBITE   To bewitch with the eye.

EYETHURL   A window.

EYNDILL   Jealous.

FADOODLE   Nonsense, something foolish.

FAFFLE   To blow in sudden gusts; to stammer or fumble. From the echoing sound of a *faff* 'gust of wind'.

FAGE   To coax, flatter, beguile.

FAIRHEAD   Beauty.

FAIRNEY-CLOOTS   Small horny substances above the hoofs of horses, sheep, and goats.

FANGER   A guardian, one who protects, as do fanged animals.

FARDRY   The act of painting the face white.

FARNET   A company of attendants.

FARTURE   Stuffing.

FARY   A state of consternation, tumult.

FASELS   Chick-peas, kidney beans.

FEARBABE   A thing designed to scare a baby.

FEAT   A dangling curl of hair.

FEATHER-HEAD   A silly, lightheaded person.

FELLOWFEEL   To share another's feelings, to sympathize with.

FELLY   Harshly, destructively.

FEWTER   A support for a lance or spear attached to a knight's saddle.

FIGGING-LAW   The practice of cutting purses and picking pockets.

FIREFANGED   Scorched; overheated and producing a singed taste or smell.

FIVE EGGS ("to come in with one's five eggs")   A sixteenth-century expression meaning to interrupt with a trivial story and to make an offer not worthwhile to the other party. From the cheap price of eggs; "to have eggs on the spit," an expression meaning very busy.

FIZGIG   A frivolous person, especially a woman. Fireworks in the form of a serpent. Paper is rolled around a roller the width of a little finger and one end of the roller is filled with fireworks material.

FLAG-FALLEN   Unemployed. From the sixteenth- and seventeenth-century custom of lowering a playhouse flag when no performance was held and the actors were out of work.

FLAP DRAGON   The sport of catching raisins in bowls of flaming brandy or drinking the brandy without getting burned as a tribute to one's mistress.

FLATCHET   A sword.

FLEAK   A pejorative term for a woman; an insignificant person.

FLERD   Deceit, fraud.

FLERK   To jerk or twitch.

FLESH-SPADES   Fingernails.

FLIPEROUS   A proud gossip, a prattler.

FLOCCINAUCINIHILIPILIFICATION (accented on *ca*)   The habit of estimating things as worthless and belittling others' achievements. A term coined by linking four words in an Eton Latin grammar book *flocci-nauci-nihili-pili-fication.* Sir Walter Scott wrote of the *floccinaucinihilipilification* of money.

FLOCKARD   A veil floating from a headdress.

FLOSH   A swamp or stagnant pool overgrown with weeds.

FNAST   To pant, snort.

FONKIN   A little fool.

FOPDOODLE   A simpleton.

FRUSH   To crush, strike, break. From the Latin *frustum* 'fragment'.

FUCUS   Rouge made from rock lichen, which produced a red dye. This false color became a cosmetic cover-up.

GANG-TEETH   Projecting teeth.

GARBOIL   Turmoil, commotion, from the Old French word *garbouille,* of the same meaning. The earlier Celtic word *garblough* meant a heavy or rough blow.

GARDYLOO   In old Edinburgh, a warning cry before throwing dirty water from windows into the street in the 1770s. From the French *gare l'eau* 'beware of the water'.

GARFANGLE HOOK   A plant reaching a height of eight feet with a hook on the top.

GATTOOTHED   Having teeth set wide apart. From the Old English *gat* 'gap'.

GIVEL   To heap up. *Giveler* was a term of contempt for a greedy person.

GLEED   Squint-eyed, one-eyed; also crooked.

GLOP   To swallow greedily; to stare at in wonder or alarm.

GOFE   The pillory.

GOLILLA   A stiff, starched collar worn in Spain in the seventeenth century. From the Latin *gula* 'throat'. Also related to gullible; capable of swallowing anything.

GRAFF   To dig.

GUNDYGUT   A glutton. Also *greedigut*.

GWENDERS   A disagreeable tingling from the cold.

HADIVIST   An expression meaning had I known, to express regret at making a mistake or letting an opportunity go by.

HA-HA   A sunken trench or ditch not visible until one steps into it. From the Anglo Saxon *hoeh* meaning hole.

HAND-BAND   A covenant made by joining hands.

HARDHEWER   A stonemason.

HEANLING   A humble or base person.

HODDYPEAK   A simpleton, blockhead.

HOFUL   Careful.

HOODPICK   A miser or skinflint.

HUDDER-MUDDER   Secrecy, privacy.

HUFTY-TUFTY   A braggart or conceited boor. Also *huff-muff, huff-snuff, huff-nose.*

HUM   A strong liquor, a mixture of ale or beer and spirits.

HURLEY-HACKET   The sport of tobogganing.

ICCHEN   To move, stir.

ILIMP   To happen, befall.

INWIT   Conscience, knowledge from within, as opposed to *outwit,* acquired knowledge.

IQUEME   Pleasing, agreeable.

IRCHIN   A hedgehog; a dish with almonds on top bearing a similarity to a hedgehog.

ISTINK   Transitive verb: to smell.

ISWONK   Toil.

JUBBE   A large vessel for liquor.

JUVAMENT   Aid!, help!

KEAK   To cackle.

KELL   A woman's headdress, cap.

KERCHIEF-OF-PLEASANCE   An embroidered cloth presented by a lady to her knight to wear for her sake. He was bound by the code of honor to put it on his helmet.

KEW-KAW   Upside-down.

KEXY   Dry, juiceless.

KIDCOTE   A prison; from the name of a specific prison in York, England.

KIDLIWINK   A beer shop, a *tidliwink*.

KILLBUCK   A fierce-looking fellow.

KILLCOW   A braggart, swashbuckler, or bully; a murderous fellow, a butcher.

KILL-PRIEST   Port wine.

KISS THE HARE'S FOOT   To be so late as to miss dinner and be able only to kiss the animal's foot; i.e., to eat left-over scraps.

KISSING-COMFITS   Sweets to make the breath pleasant.

KNOSP   An architectural ornament in the form of a bud or knob.

LANDCHEAP   A fine paid to the lord of a manor when leaving his land.

LENNOW   Flabby, limp.

LICKSPIGOT   One who fawns or behaves in a servile manner. Also *lickspittle, lickdish*.

LIFTING MONDAY   Easter Monday in the 1800s, when it was the custom in Lancashire for men to lift up and kiss each woman they met. On Easter Tuesday women could do likewise for the men. The custom was stopped because of the disturbances it caused.

LINESEAT   A stool to use while spinning.

LIP-CLAP   Kissing.

LIRIPOOP A tail that hung from a graduate's hood, the precursor of the modern tassel on a mortarboard; a decorative scarf; a storehouse of knowledge; a role or part, something to be learned; a trick, or a silly person.

LOVECUP A local market duty, tax.

LOVE DAYS Certain days appointed to settle differences between parties by amicable arbitration.

LOVEDRURY A keepsake, love token.

LUBBER-WORT Food or drink that makes one idle and stupid. Food of no nutritional value, "junk food."

LULIBUB Early form of *lollipop*.

MAGSMAN A swindler.

MAILY Speckled.

MALLY Foolishly fond.

MALSHAVE Caterpillar.

MASTIGADOUR A watering bit for a horse.

MAW-WALLOP A badly cooked mess of food.

MELPOMENISH (accent on *pom*) Tragic. From Melpomene, the Greek muse of tragedy.

MENTIMUTATION A change of mind.

MERRY-GALL A sore produced by chafing.

MERRY-GO-DOWN Strong ale.

MERRY-GO-SORRY A tale that evokes mixed feelings of joy and sorrow.

MILDFUL Merciful.

MISGLOZE To misinterpret.

MOBARD   Clown, boor. A term of contempt.

MUBBLEFUBBLES   A depression of the spirits for no reason, melancholy. Also *blue devils, mulligrubs.*

MUCKENDER   A bib or handkerchief.

MULWINE   A drinking bout.

MUMPER   A beggar, one who sponges off others.

MUMPOKER   A word used to frighten naughty children.

MUNG   Food for chickens; a crowd of people.

MURFLES   Freckles, pimples.

NABCHEAT   A hat, cap.

NESH   Fresh, delicate, soft; applied to fruit, vegetables, and foliage.

NICKPOT   A fraudulent innkeeper.

NITHE   Envy, hatred.

NOSE OF WAX   A fickle personality, anything accommodating; also, applied to one's flexibility of faith as a means of protecting oneself; and also to describe Catholic writers who variously interpreted the Holy Scriptures.

NOTT-HEADED, NOTT-PATED   Having hair closely cut, from the Saxon *hnot.*

NYLE   Fog, mist.

ODAM (accent on *o*)   A son-in-law.

ODDWOMAN   A female umpire or arbitrator.

OKSELLE   Armpit.

ONGLE   Claw.

ONG-TONGUE   See *blob-tale.*

OPEN-TIDE   Early spring, the time when buds open.

ORLINGS   Teeth of a comb.

ORMUZINE   A fabric brought from Ormuz, near the entrance to the Persian Gulf, in the 1600s.

OUTWIT   Knowledge, information, learning one gains from outside oneself.

PAGGLE   To bulge, hang loosely.

PANCART   A placard with public notices.

PASH   The forehead. From the Gaelic *bash* or *pash,* the root word for *abash,* browbeat, intimidate.

PENISTONE (pronounced *pennistun*)   Coarse woollen cloth woven in the town of Penistone, England.

PHILOTIMY   Love of honor.

PINGLE   To eat with very little appetite.

PISSABED   A name given to the dandelion for its diuretic effects.

PITCHKETTLED   Puzzled, from the Scotch word *kittled.*

POOP-NODDY   A fool or simpleton; the game of love.

POPLOLLY   A little darling (from the French *poupelet*); a female favorite, special loved one, or mistress.

PORKNELL   One as fat as a pig.

PRICKMEDAINTY   A dandy, a person of either sex who is finicky about his or her style of dress. From one meaning of *prick,* which is to pin somebody up, thus to dress up elaborately. John Skelton wrote a ridiculing verse, "The Tunnying of Elynour Rummyng," in 1829.

PRICK-SONG   A song in which the notes were written (*pricked*) down, as opposed to a plain-song, which was not recorded; also harmony.

PUDDING-PRICK   A slender wooden skewer with which the ends of gut containing pudding were fastened.

PUMPKINIFICATION   Pompous behavior or exaggerated praise. From incorrect Greek translation of a word meaning divinity in a text by Seneca.

PURFLE   To decorate, adorn.

QUETCH   To moan and twitch in pain, shake.

QUOP   To throb, palpitate.

REAKS   Pranks, practical jokes.

RECOOPER   Recovery.

REDMOD   Hasty, rash.

REELPOT   One who makes a drinking pot go around.

RIBBLE   A wrinkle, furrow.

RIDING THE STANG   A form of public ridicule formerly practiced in parts of England, Scotland, and Wales to punish a husband for beating or betraying his wife. A parade was formed in which the guilty party was carried through the streets and denounced by the populace or exposed to humiliation through derisive verse. See *skimmington*.

RINGO   A treat; a sweet made from the candied root of the sea holly, supposed to be an aphrodisiac.

RIXLE   To rule, have dominion.

ROAKY   Hazy, nebulous, not clear, from the French word *rauque,* pertaining to the voice, meaning hoarse or thick.

ROBERDAVY   A kind of wine in the sixteenth and seventeenth centuries.

ROOPED   Hoarse, as with bronchitis or a throat cold.

RUBB   A seal or sea dog from Greenland.

RUMFORDIZE   To improve a smoky chimney according to a system invented by Sir Benjamin Thompson, the Count von Rumford, in the early 1800s.

RUTTERKIN   A swaggering gallant or bully.

SAMDED   Half-dead. From the Old English *sam* and the Latin *semi.*

SANAP   A strip of cloth placed over the outer part of tablecloth to keep it from being soiled.

SCRIBBET   Charcoal for drawing.

SCROGGLINGS   Small, worthless apples left hanging on a tree after the crop is gathered.

SCROW   The sky.

SCRUBBADO (accent on *ba*)   "The itch."

SHAB   To get rid of, to put something over on someone.

'SHEART   A euphemistic shortening of *God's heart,* an oath.

SHITEROW (long *i*)   A heron.

SHITTLE   Unstable, inconstant. From the Old English *sceotan* 'to run hastily'.

SHONGABLE   A tax on making certain shoes, in the 1400s.

SKIMMINGTON   A form of public ridicule practiced in the south of England to punish a husband for beating or betraying his wife. It consisted of a parade in which actors impersonating husband and wife rode through town on a donkey or in a cart beating each other with ladles or skimming spoons. See *riding the stang.*

SLIBBER-SAUCE   A nauseating concoction especially for medicinal purposes.

SLOOMY   Lazy, dull, sleepy.

SMELLSMOCK   A licentious man, a derogatory term for such priests.

SNAPSAUCE   Pilfering food; licking one's fingers.

SNAWK   To smell.

SNIRTLE   To snicker, to laugh quietly and mockingly.

SNOT   The burnt part of a candlewick, not a vulgar term in the fifteenth through seventeenth centuries.

SNOTTER-CLOUT   A pocket handkerchief.

SPARPLE   To scatter, spread about.

SPARROW-FART   Daybreak, very early morning.

SPERLING   A small fish, probably the European smelt, *Osmerus eperlanus;* a young American herring.

SPISS   Thick, dense.

SPITCHCOCK   Eel cooked with bread crumbs; quickly cut and cooked fowl, a quick dish for unexpected guests. From *despatchcock.*

SPIT-FROG   A small sword, a term of contempt.

SPITTLE   A hospital for lower-class indigents and lepers where they were housed but not necessarily cured.

SPOUSEBREAK   See *bedswerver.*

SPUDDLE   To assume airs of importance without reason; to make trifles seem important.

SQUECK   A disease affecting fowl.

SQUIDDLE   To waste time with idle talk.

SQUINT-A-PIPES   Slang for a squinting man or woman.

STEVEN   The voice, a loud outcry; a set time, appointment.

STOOP-GALLANT   Something that humbles the great and makes one a mere man; an early sixteenth-century name for a quick, fatal fever, the "sweating sickness."

STORGE (pronounced "stor'gee")   Natural love, especially of parents for their children. From the Greek *stergein* 'to love'.

STRAIGHT-FINGERED   Thoroughly honest, having fingers that won't bend to hold dishonest gains.

STREETMAN   An official appointed for the good government of the London streets.

SUGGILL   To beat black and blue; to defame.

SWARF-PENNY   Dues paid in commutation of the services of a castle guard.

SWELCHIE   A whirlpool. From the Old Norse *swelgan* 'swallow, devour' and the Old English *geswelg* 'abyss'.

SWERKED   To become troubled, gloomy. From the Old Saxon *swerkan.*

TABLINGHOUSE   A gambling house.

TAW-BESS   A slut, slattern.

TEAR CAT   A seventeenth-century term to criticize ranting actors who overdid their parts.

TEENFUL   Troublesome, irritating.

TENTERBELLY   A glutton.

THEEK   To cover a roof with straw thatch; to protect.

THEOW   A servant, slave.

THIBBLE   A stick for stirring porridge.

THIGGING   Begging.

THRING   Verb: to press, crush; noun: a throng.

THRIP   To snap one's fingers.

THRUNCH   Very angry, displeased.

TIDLIWINK   A tavern, possibly where the game of tid-liwinks arose; a *kidliwink.*

TINGLE-NAIL   The smallest kind of tack, a nail about one-quarter inch long.

TIPSYCAKE   Cake saturated with wine or liquor, stuck with almonds, and served with custard.

TIRLIRY-PUFFKIN   Light-headed, flighty woman, a flirt.

TITIVIL   A name for the devil, who steals words

dropped during the recitation of a service so the name can be used later against the offender; a knave, a tattler. From *Titivillus,* the devil, a word created by monks in mystery plays.

TITTUP   The canter of a horse, onomatopoetic from the sound of a horse's feet; to walk up and down in prancing movements; a forward woman, a hussy.

TRANTLES   Articles of little value.

TRUCKS   A game adapted from an Italian game like billiards. The English game had an upright form called a king placed at one end of table, to which one rolled balls over a board with thirteen holes in it.

TRUE-HEAD   Fidelity.

TRUNDLE-TAIL   A low-bred dog.

TURNGIDDY   Dizzy.

TUSHES   See *wang-tooth.*

TUTMOUTHED   Having protruding lips or a projecting lower jaw.

TUZZY-MUZZY   A nosegay of flowers. From the Old English *tus* 'cluster, knot'. Also *tisty-tosty.*

UG   Fear, dread.

UMBECAST   To consider or ponder. From the Old English *ymbe* 'around'; to surround, encircle.

UPSY   In the style of.

VASQUINE   A petticoat.

VECKE   An old woman.

VELLICATION   A twitching or convulsive movement.

VELVET HEAD   A term of contempt. From the head of a young deer, whose horns are covered with "velvet."

VENENATE   To poison.

VERME   A legendary fish from Ganges that was able to seize and destroy elephants.

VOIL   A town.

WAGHALTER   A rogue likely to swing in a gallows.

WALKING MORT   A grown-up unmarried whore, who often pretends to be a widow.

WALLYDRAIGLE   A worthless, slovenly woman.

WAM   A scar, cicatrix.

WANG-TOOTH   A molar. From the Old English *wang* 'to the side'. A *wang-tooth* is situated next to the *tushes* 'tusks'.

WELKIN   A sky with woolly clouds. From the Saxon *wealcan* 'to roll', *wolke* 'cloud', and the German *wolle* 'wool'.

WHEEPLE   An ineffectual attempt of a man to whistle loudly. An onomatopoetic term, from the low cheep of a bird.

WHIFLING   An insignificant creature.

WHIPPERGINNIE   An abusive term for a woman. The land of *whipperginnie* became a nickname for purgatory and a card game. Also *whip-her-jenny*.

WHISTERSNEFET   A blow to the ear. Also *whisterpoop*.

WHITELIVER   A coward.

WHOOPUBB   A hubbub.

WIDDERSHINS   Unlucky, prone to misfortune.

WIND-SUCKER   An envious, covetous person. A *yisser.*
This term originally referred to a species of hawk that
feeds on mice and hovers greedily, almost motionless,
in the air over its prey. Chapman used the term to
criticize Ben Jonson in the preface to his *Iliad,* saying,
"There is a certain envious *wind-sucker* that hovers up
and down, laboriously ingrossing all the air with his
luxurious ambition."

WINK-A-PEEPS   Eyes.

WINX   To bray, as an ass.

WONG   Meadowlands, commons.

WOODNESS   Madness, insanity. From the Old English
wood 'out of one's mind.'

WOUP   A hoop or ring, especially of plain metal, unset
with stones.

WURP   A stone's throw; a glance of the eye.

XENODOCHIAL   Hospitable to strangers.

XIPH   A swordfish.

YARKEN   To prepare.

YCORE   Chosen, elect.

YEPSEN   Cupping the hands, and as much as the hands
will hold. From the Old English *geap* 'open,' and
gowpen, 'curved'.

YERD   To beat with a rod.

YERESYEVE   A gift given at the new year or upon taking office.

YETTER   A caster of metal.

YISSER   See *wind-sucker.*

YOUNGHEDE   A youth.

YUKY (pronounced *yooky*)   Itchy.

ZARF   A cup, especially one made of ornamental metal in Arabic countries. Also a cup-shaped holder for hot coffee.

ZEGEDINE   A drinking cup.

ZENDALET   A large, black, square, wool shawl folded into a triangle to be worn over the shoulders or on a wire frame on the head in eighteenth-century Venice. The word came to mean gondolas themselves, since the cloth trailed into the water.

ZOPISSA   An old medicinal application made from wax and pitch scraped from the sides of ships so coated as to harden and protect the metal.

ZUCHE   A tree stump.

fellowfeeling

Bibliography

Andrews, William. *Old-Time Punishments.* London: The Tabard Press Ltd., 1890.

Armour, J. S. *The Genesis and Growth of English.* New York: Oxford University Press, 1935.

Barnett, Lincoln. *The Treasure of Our Tongue.* New York: Alfred Knopf, 1964.

Brewer, E. Cobham. *Dictionary of Phrase and Fable.* Philadelphia: Henry Altemus Co., 1898.

Davies, T. Lewis. *A Supplementary English Glossary.* London: George Bell and Sons, 1881.

Halliwell-Philips, James Orchard. 7th ed. *A Dictionary of Archaic and Provincial Words, Obsolete Phrases, Proverbs and Ancient Customs from the Fourteenth Century.* 2 vols. London: George Routledge and Sons, 1924.

Mackay, Charles. *A Glossary of Obscure Words in the Writings of Shakespeare and his Contemporaries.* London: Gilbert and Rivington, Ltd., 1887.

————. *The Lost Beauties of the English Language, an appeal to authors, poets, clergymen, and public speakers.* New York: Bouton, 1874.

Murray, James A. H.; Bradley, Henry; Craigie, W. A.; and Onions, C. T. *The Oxford English Dictionary.* 12 vols. Oxford: The Clarendon Press, 1933.

Nares, Robert. *A Glossary of Words, Phrases, Names, and Allusions in Works of English Authors, Particularly of Shakespeare and His Contemporaries.* London: George Routledge and Sons, 1905.

Reid, Alastair. *Ounce, Dice, Trice.* Boston: Little, Brown, & Co., 1958.

Shipley, Joseph T. *Dictionary of Early English.* New York: Philosophical Library, 1955.

Skeat, Walter William. *A Glossary of Tudor and Stuart Words, especially from the dramatists.* Oxford: The Clarendon Press, 1914.

Toone, William. *A Glossary and Etymological Dictionary of Obsolete and Uncommon Words.* London: Wm. Pickering, 1832.

Wright, Thomas. *Dictionary of Obsolete and Provincial English.* 2 vols. London: Henry G. Bohn, 1857.